Test Your
Business English
Finance

CW00742962

Simon Sweeney

Series Editor: Nick Brieger

To Judith, Ruth and Neil, with love from Dad.

Pearson Education Limited
Edinburgh Gate
Harlow
Essex
CM20 2JE
England

ISBN 0 582 46115 4

This edition first published 2000
First published in Penguin Books 1997

Copyright © Simon Sweeney 1997, 2000
Illustrations copyright © Neville Swaine 1997

The moral right of the author and of the illustrator has been asserted.

Test Your... series developed by Peter Watcyn-Jones

Printed in Spain by Mateu Cromo, S. A. Pinto (Madrid)

All rights reserved: no part of this publication may be reproduced, stored in a retrieval system, or transmitted in any form or by any means, electronic, mechanical, photocopying, recording or otherwise, without the prior written permission of the Publishers.

Published by Pearson Education Limited in association with Penguin Books Ltd, both companies being subsidiaries of Pearson plc.

Acknowledgements
The author would like to thank Simon Blackley for help with source material. Thanks too, to my colleague and editor Nick Brieger for, as always, constructive, concise and cogent criticism. Finally, thanks to Michael Nation and colleagues at Penguin Longman Publishing.

INTRODUCTION

Language knowledge and communication skills are the basic tools for developing competence in a foreign language. Vocabulary, together with a command of grammar and pronunciation, are the main components of language knowledge.

This series aims to develop the vocabulary required by professionals and pre-service students. The materials provide clear and simple test materials of around 500 key concepts and terms in various professional areas. Each book is devoted to one professional area, divided into eight sections. Each section, focusing on one topic area, tests the knowledge of both concepts and terms. The materials can be used as part of a language course for specialists or as a handy reference for self-study.

For the first books, we have chosen areas which are of significant current interest in the business world. Each has been written by an author with considerable practical experience in the field and we hope that the series will prove a valuable aid to users.

ABOUT THIS BOOK

Test Your Business English: Finance is for two groups of learners: learners of Finance English at intermediate level; learners of general English who want to develop their knowledge of Finance English. In both cases, it aims to help them:
• check their knowledge of core concepts and key terms (words and expressions) used in finance
• see how these terms are used so that they can use them effectively and successfully themselves.

The book will also be a useful source of information for trainers who need to run courses in Finance English at intermediate level.

The material has been designed for self-study or classroom use.

Organization of the material

The book is divided into eight sections and each section deals with a different area of Finance English. In this way it is organized more like a textbook than a testbook, with individual sections devoted to individual areas. We have chosen to do this so that, if they wish, learners can work through each section and see how terms group together. We believe this will help learners develop their range of expression in a structured and systematic way.

After the tests, there is a complete answer key followed by a full multilingual A–Z word list.

Using the material

The Contents page shows the eight main areas covered. Learners can either work through the book from the beginning or select chapters according to their interests or needs. After each test, learners should check their answers. While working on a test, learners may come across unknown or unfamiliar words. This is an opportunity for them to check their understanding and extend their knowledge. So, a good dictionary of general English, as well as a more specialist dictionary, will be useful companions to this volume. In this way the material in this book can be used both for testing and for teaching.

Selection of the terms

The terms are directly relevant to the work of people working in finance. General terms are not included, nor are very technical terms. Only in section 1 are more basic terms included where we think that their understanding is important to the understanding of other more specialised terms. Finally, the language model is predominantly British English.

Other titles in the series

Test Your Business English: *General Usage*

Test Your Business English: *Elementary*

Test Your Business English: *Intermediate*

Test Your Business English: *Hotel and Catering*

Test Your Business English: *Marketing*

Test Your Business English: *Secretarial*

Test Your Business English: *Accounting*

(Each of these books tests core vocabulary in their respective areas.)

CONTENTS

1 Who's who in finance

Match each job title on the left with the correct definition on the right (a–j). Use the grid below. (See example):

1 tax inspector

2 tax consultant

3 bank manager

4 commodity trader

5 accountant

6 finance director

7 market analyst

8 financial advisor

9 insurance broker

10 stockbroker

a) The person who is responsible for an individual bank.

b) Someone who advises people on how to manage their financial affairs.

c) Someone who prepares an individual's (or a company's) tax return.

d) The person who is responsible for the financial side of running a business.

e) A government official who checks that you are paying enough tax.

f) The person who finds you the best insurance policy at the best price.

g) Someone who buys and sells stocks and shares for clients, and charges a commission.

h) Someone who advises you or a company on how to pay less tax.

i) Someone who comments on business and share prices in a particular sector of the economy.

j) Someone who buys and sells things in large quantities, especially food products such as tea, coffee, cereals, and other raw materials.

1	2	3	4	5	6	7	8	9	10
e									

2 What's what in finance

Match each word on the left with the correct definition on the right (a–o). Use the grid below. (See example):

1 pension

2 bank

3 tax

4 dividends

5 shares

6 inflation

7 bankruptcy

8 capital spending

9 profit

10 interest

11 assets

12 turnover

13 liabilities

14 accounts

15 mortgage

a) Something that the government collects and no one likes to pay.

b) Where you go to borrow money or get cash.

c) How you are charged for borrowing money.

d) How you can pay to buy a house, unless you can pay for it in a single payment.

e) A type of investment made by a company when buying equipment.

f) What, in financial terms, a business hopes to make.

g) What a company has to prepare every year for presentation to its owners and to the relevant authorities.

h) The situation where a company does not have enough money or property to pay its debts, and so the company closes.

i) The total amount of sales in a year.

j) Rising prices, rising costs and rising wages in an economy.

k) What you buy if you invest money in a company.

l) Individuals who invest their money in a company hope to receive these regularly.

m) When you are old, you hope to have one of these.

n) The name for all the property, equipment, investments and money owned by a company (or individual).

o) The name for everything that a company owes.

1	2	3	4	5	6	7	8	9	10	11	12	13	14	15
m														

3 Word families

Financial vocabulary covers several areas, including economics, banking, marketing, personal finance and financial planning. Here is a selection of key words. Complete the table.

	Verb	**Personal noun**	**General noun**	**Adjective**
1	to analyze			
2		competitor		
3			advice	–
4	to merge	–		
5	to industrialize			
6		trader		
7				exporting/exported
8		producer		
9		supplier		
10		consumer		
11	to guarantee			
12	to credit			
13			debit	
14		earner		
15		investor		

4 Pictures used in talking about finance

Pictures often help to make information clearer. This test introduces language used to describe pictures of financial data. Match the words below with the correct numbers in the pictures.

pie chart	table	line graph .....
histogram/bar graph	segment	row .....
column	vertical axis	horizontal axis .....
broken line	solid line	dotted line .....
undulating line	fluctuating line	curve .....

Balance in working capital

	Jan	Feb	Mar
Assets			
Cash	41,360	36,320	40,301
Accounts receivable	515,420	596,319	502,736
Inventory	163,200	189,850	143,220
Liabilities			
Accounts payable	141,251	138,890	111,201
Net working capital	578,729	683,599	686,257

1 ....

2 ....

3 ....

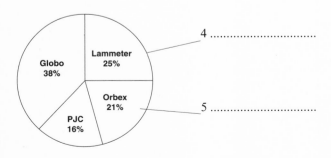

Globo 38%

Lammeter 25%

Orbex 21%

PJC 16%

4 ....

5 ....

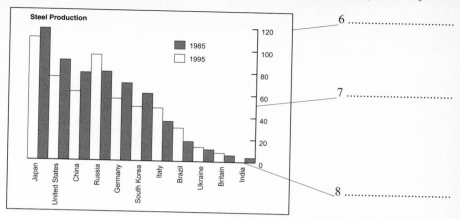

6 ....

7 ....

8 ....

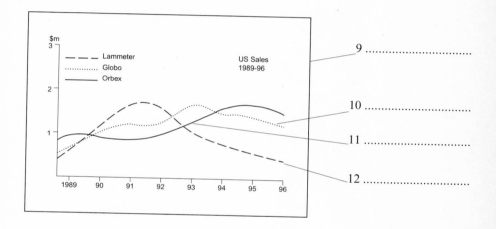

9 ....

10 ....

11 ....

12 ....

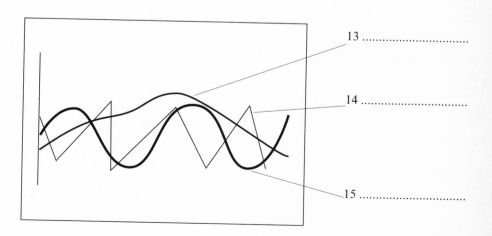

13 ....

14 ....

15 ....

5 Financial documents

Match each word on the left with the correct definition on the right (a–i). Use the grid below. (See example):

1 profit and loss account

2 balance sheet

3 cash budget

4 share certificate

5 tender

6 business plan

7 insurance certificate

8 letter of credit

9 contract

a) A plan of cash income and cash spending for a specific period of time.

b) A document which represents a part of the total stock value of a company and which shows who owns it.

c) A formal agreement to provide goods or services.

d) A formal description of income and costs for a time period that has finished.

e) A formal description of a company's financial position at a specified moment.

f) A document which states that a named person has paid for protection against accidental loss or damage of goods or property.

g) A description of the ways a new business hopes to make money, showing possible income and expenditure.

h) A formal letter with an offer to supply goods or services, containing a description of the project, including costs, materials, personnel, time plans, etc.

i) An official notification from a bank that it will lend money to a customer.

1	2	3	4	5	6	7	8	9
d								

6 Describing trends 1

There are many ways to describe change. This test looks at several alternatives.

A Give the opposite to each of the following:

rise/ _ _ _ _   increase/_ _ _ _ _ _ _ _   go up/_ _ _ _ _ _

climb/_ _ _ _ _ _ _   shrink/_ _ _ _ _ _   deteriorate/_ _ _ _ _ _ _

get better/_ _ _ _ _ _ _ _   collapse/_ _ _ _ _ _ _ _   hit bottom/ _ _ _ _

B Match each word or phrase in the box to one of the graphs (1–9) below. Look at the line between the two crosses. (See example):

decline to nothing .7..	collapse	stay the same .....
reach a peak	edge down	recover .....
increase steadily	fluctuate	rise slightly .....

①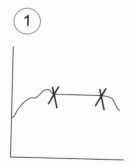

②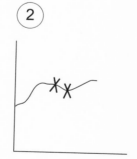

③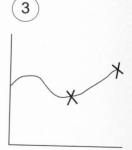

7

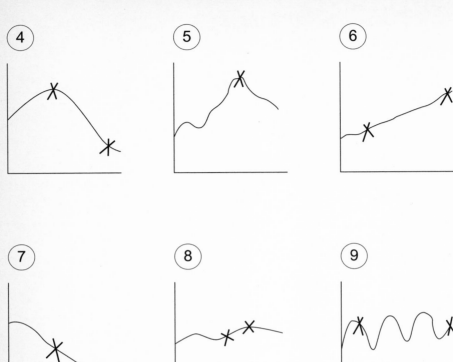

7 Types of company

There are five main types of legally constituted company. Each type of company has different characteristics. Tick the correct characteristics for each business type, or write 'possibly' if the characteristic could apply.

	SINGLE INDIVIDUAL OWNS COMPANY	TWO OR MORE OWNERS/ DIRECTORS	QUOTED ON STOCK EXCHANGE	WORKERS RUN THE COMPANY	UNLIMITED LIABILITY	LIMITED LIABILITY	OWNER IS SELF- EMPLOYED
PUBLIC LIMITED COMPANY							
PRIVATE LIMITED COMPANY							
SOLE TRADER							
PARTNERSHIP							
CO-OPERATIVE							

8 Common acronyms and abbreviations

What do the following abbreviations mean? Fill in the missing letters.

1 VAT   Value A _ _ _ _   T _ _

2 PLC   Public L _ _ _ _ _ _   C _ _ _ _ _ _

3 Ltd   L _ _ _ _ _ _

4 & Co.   _ _ _ _ _ _ _ _ _ y

5 CWO   C _ _ _ W _ _ _   Order

6 COD   Cash O _ D _ _ _ _ _ _ _

7 c.i.f.   c _ _ _ , i _ _ _ _ _ _ _ _ , freight

8 PAYE   Pay A _ Y _ _ E _ _ _ (i.e. tax)

9 p/e ratio   p _ _ _ _/earnings r _ _ _ _

10 P & L account.   P _ _ _ _ _ and L _ _ _ account

9 Introducing key terms in financial planning

Complete the sentences below with a word from the box.

break-even point	gross profit margin	profitability	turnover
core activity	net profit margin	selling costs	
cost of sales	overheads	setting-up costs	

1 .... shows how a business might make profits. It is calculated from the relationship between profit and the capital invested in the company, and between profit and turnover.

2 The .... of a business is the total amount of sales, before costs are deducted.

3 The .... of a business is the main product or service which the business provides, e.g. for FIAT it is cars.

4 The .... is the profit the business makes before costs are considered.

5 The .... are the costs involved in creating a new business.

6 The .... are the normal costs of a business, which do not change if production rises. They are also referred to as indirect costs or fixed costs.

7 The .... is a calculation of profit after deducting the cost of sales and overheads.

8 The .... are all the costs directly associated with producing the products.

9 The .... is the amount of sales a company needs to cover all costs.

10 The .... are all costs directly concerned with getting customers to buy products and moving them to the customer.

10 Costs? What costs?

Put the terms in the box under the correct heading, then match them to the correct picture (1–7).

labour costs	production costs	advertising costs	distribution costs
storage costs	selling costs	administrative costs	

Fixed costs   **Variable costs**

....

....

....

                                                ....

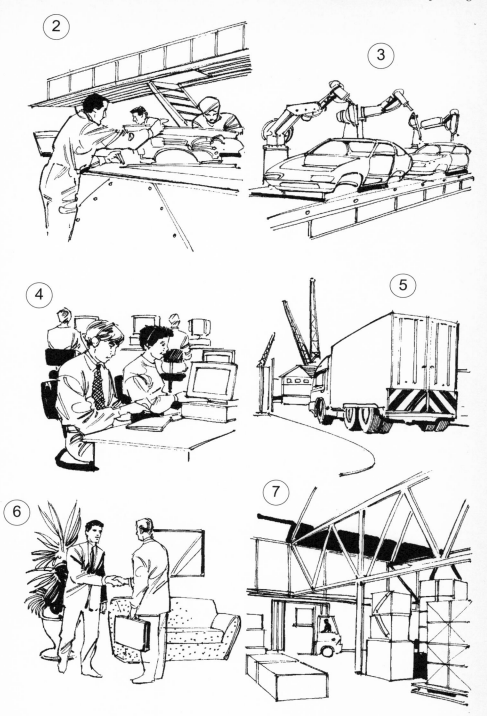

11 Identifying costs

Read the definitions below, then complete the phrases that follow by combining an appropriate word from the box with *cost(s)*.

price	fixed	variable	centre	analysis
manufacturing	operating	labour	selling	sales

1 Usual expenses such as rent, heating, lighting, which are not changed by the volume of production. .... costs

2 Expenses which increase with increased production, e.g. labour, raw materials. .... costs

3 All costs directly related to production. .... costs

4 All costs directly related to getting someone to buy a product. .... costs

5 The cost of employing workers and staff. .... costs

6 The costs for the day-to-day running of a company or business. .... costs

7 Selling at a price which is exactly what the product has cost to make. cost ....

8 The study of all likely costs associated with a product. cost ....

9 A business in a chain, or a subsidiary, but treated as independent for accounting. cost ....

10 The total costs for all products sold. cost of ....

12 What's a master budget?

Here is part of a description of a master budget, given in a class to management trainees. Complete the spaces with appropriate words from the box.

administrative	cash	income	turnover
budget	fixed	raw	variable
capital	forecast	sheet	

In business planning, a company financial controller needs to prepare a master budget. This is a budgeted (1) .... statement which shows (2) .... income and expenditure, and also a balance (3) ....

   The master budget summarizes various forecasts, or budgets. Each of the following needs its own (4) .... : sales, showing expected (5) .... , production, showing all overheads and costs, both (6) .... and (7) .... , e.g. labour, (8) .... materials and components. A separate (9) .... expenditure budget shows major spending on equipment and machinery. Another budget shows all general and (10) .... expenditure that the business needs. Also, a (11) .... budget shows estimated income and expenditure of cash, i.e. not cheque or credit card payments or payments by banker's order.

13 Cash terms

Read the definitions below, then complete the phrases that follow by combining an appropriate word from the box with *cash*.

advance	delivery	hard	price	settlement
budget	flow	petty	ready	

1 Small amounts of money in notes and coins for regular, ... cash
small purchases.

2 Money in notes and coins, not cheques or credit card transfers. .... cash

3 Cash which comes in to a company from sales, after costs, cash ....
overheads, etc.

4 Payment when the customer receives the goods. cash on ....

5 Plan of cash income and expenditure. cash ....

6 A loan in cash against a future payment. cash ....

7 Notes and coins available for immediate expenditure. .... cash

8 Payment of a bill with cash. cash ....

9 A low price for payment in cash. cash ....

14 Sales forecasting

Sales forecasting is based on a variety of estimates, depending on the product or service concerned and the market involved.

A Below is part of a report by Michelle Cardot, the Marketing Manager of Fastrail Ltd, an urban transport system operator. Put the five parts of the report in the correct order.

1

> The sales forecaster interviews sales staff, sales managers and senior management. Talking with experts and analysing figures from previous years helps to show trends, the relationship between price and demand, and any seasonal variations. The forecaster also considers the effects of advertising, or changes in the market. For example, if new competition arrives or old competitors disappear.

2

> ## 4.2 Sales forecasting
>
> Sales forecasting is an attempt to estimate the level of regular business. It includes existing contracts, the typical volume of sales to regular customers, typical volume of non-regular business and an estimate of the volume of new business.

3

> Sales volume will be affected by the effectiveness of advertising and other promotional activities, the quality of the sales force, past sales volume and any seasonal influences.

4

> Pricing policy is affected by market conditions, competition, economic climate, industrial conditions and organizational cost structure.

5

> Factors affecting sales forecasting include pricing policy and sales volume.

report

B Here is a memo based on the same report. Put the five sections of the memo into the correct order.

1
> *Factors affecting pricing policy:*
> market conditions, competition, economic climate, industrial conditions and organizational cost structure.

2
> Forecasting uses personal interviews with both staff and management and also analysis of past sales figures. The relationship between price and demand can also be significant.
> At all times, forecasts can be adjusted, depending on changes.

3
> *Factors affecting sales volume:*
> advertising, promotional activities, quality of sales force, past sales volume and seasonal variation.

4
> # *Fastrail Ltd*
> ## INTERNAL MEMO
>
> From: Michelle Cardot – Marketing Director
> To: JT, DS, HR, PD, PV
> Date: 22 October 20..
>
> **Subject: Sales forecasting**
>
> Sales forecasting estimates the level of future business, combining volume of sales to regular customers with non-regular business and probable demand from new business.

5
> **Factors affecting sales forecasting:**
> pricing policy and sales volume.

memo

15 Price-demand relationship

Read the newspaper article below about a truck manufacturer. Then find words or phrases in the text which mean more or less the same as the phrases given on the next page.

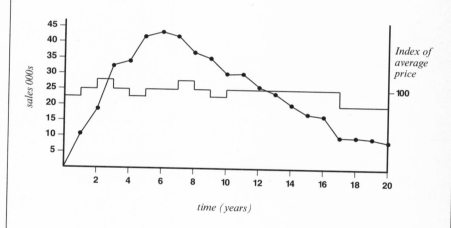

The Crown slips –
US truck giant drops top seller

time (years)

FD Auto, the largest independent truck manufacturer in the USA, yesterday announced plans to end production of its biggest-selling truck, the Crown 5000. Over half a million Crown trucks have been sold in 20 years, but sales in the past five years have declined to only 9,000 last year.

Three years ago the company cut prices by 20% to try to stimulate demand but sales rose by less than 5%. The price cut ate up the entire margin. Even in the normally price-sensitive US truck market, the Crown could not recover.

'It's a sad day, but we have to face reality. The Crown has passed its sell-by-date,' said Laurie Seller, the Marketing Manager for FD Auto. He accepted that the price cut had failed, saying that the company had miscalculated. 'Demand for the Crown is now totally inelastic: price does not affect demand. It's a dead truck. We cannot make any profit.'

It is not all bad news for FD Auto, however. Annual sales showed a small increase and turnover is expected to rise in the components division.

1 consumers wanting to buy the product

2 difference between cost price and selling price

3 easily influenced by price changes

4 old-fashioned

5 reduction in price

6 not affected by price changes

7 sales in a year

8 total sales

16 Key terms in managing company finances

A Match the phrases on the left with a word or phrase on the right which means the same.

1 contribution ratio	a) turnover
2 fixed costs	b) gross profit margin
3 variable costs	c) overheads
4 income from sales	d) direct costs

B Match the term on the left with an appropriate definition on the right.

1 contribution	a) The number or total value of sales necessary to equal all costs.
2 capital costs	b) Net value of a company (total assets less total liabilities).
3 gearing	c) Net profit available for reinvestment in the company.
4 retained profit	d) Sales income less variable costs.
5 work-in-progress	e) Selling price less variable costs divided by volume of production.
6 wealth	f) Cost of buying fixed assets such as buildings, equipment, vehicles.
7 unit contribution	g) Relationship between the cost of borrowing money and the total equity capital.
8 break-even point	h) Work done which has cost the company but has not yet been sold.

17 Setting up a business: the contribution factor

Look at the four formulae below.

Contribution = sales revenue - variable costs.
Profit = Total value of contributions - total costs

or

Profit = Revenue - {variable costs + fixed costs}

$$\text{Break-even volume of production} = \frac{\text{fixed costs}}{\text{unit contribution}}$$

The conversation below is between a tutor and a student in a seminar on setting up in business. Complete the spaces.

Teacher: All products sold should make a *contribution* to the business.

Student: What is contribution?

Teacher: It is the selling price of goods sold by the company: (1) .... ; less (2) ....

Student: So, it's like margin.

Teacher: Yes, it's the same as the gross profit margin. But, to calculate profit, you have to consider (3) .... costs. In other words, the total value of contributions less (4) .... and (5) .... costs.

Student: I see. And when you've made enough contributions, you reach your break-even point.

Teacher: Yes, that's right. Then you start to make profit.

Student: How do you calculate the break-even point?

Teacher: You have to divide the (6) .... by the (7) .... , or the contribution made by a single item that you sell.

Student: So if you raise your price, you increase the value of the contributions.

Teacher: Yes, but you must not raise your price so much that you lose sales.

18 Overheads

Here is a list of 16 fixed cost items. Categorize them according to the headings given below.

electricity account	professional indemnity insurance
employer's liability insurance	books, newspapers
mortgage payments	rent
salaries	leasing of computers
telephone	car and van hire
car hire purchase agreements	employee national insurance contributions
secretarial support	accountancy fees
stationery and printing	equipment, machinery

Services

....

....

Property

....

....

Employee costs

....

....

Equipment

....

....

Miscellaneous fixed costs

....

....

Insurance

....

....

Vehicles

....

....

Administration

....

Professional fees

....

19 Cashflow problems and other difficulties

Choose the correct definition for each of the terms in *italic*.

1 *cashflow*

   a) money from sales and money going out to meet costs, both fixed and variable

   b) cash available to pay debts

   c) payment of fixed costs, including salaries

2 *to reschedule overdraft payments*

   a) stop paying overdraft credits to the bank

   b) set a new level of payments and/or change the frequency of payments to the bank

   c) ask the bank for a bigger loan

3 *liquidity problem*

   a) not paying debts

   b) customers who are late in making payments

   c) not enough cash available to pay for costs

4 *liquid assets*

   a) wealth that can easily be changed into cash

   b) property that cannot be easily changed into cash

   c) stocks and shares in drinks companies

5 *bad debts*

   a) large bills to pay

   b) old invoices that the customer has not paid

   c) customers who always pay late

6 *to go into liquidation*

    a) to have a lot of money, especially cash

    b) to go bankrupt and to stop trading

    c) to be taken over by another company

7 *to record a credit deficit*

    a) to have no profits

    b) to be refused credit by a supplier

    c) to make a loss

8 *debit balance*

    a) the same as a credit deficit

    b) debits and credits are equal

    c) the number of debits is the same as the company forecast

9 *capacity problem*

    a) workers are not able to meet production needs

    b) the company is already producing the maximum quantity possible, but there is demand for more

    c) costs are at the maximum level the company can afford and the bank will not lend any more money

10 *opportunity cost*

    a) the costs associated with doing new business

    b) the cost of *not* doing something

    c) the cost of research and development

20 Working out the break-even point

Look at the diagram below showing the break-even point for a business. Then complete the description below using words from the box.

break-even point	loss	sales revenue	variable costs
fixed costs	profit	total costs	

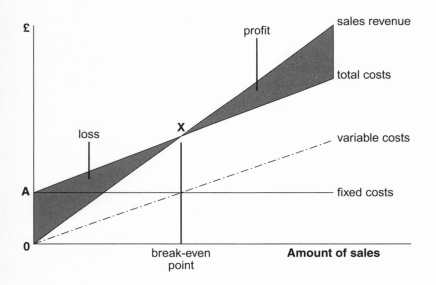

The horizontal line shows (1) .... The dotted line which starts at point 0 shows the (2).......................... for different levels of sales. The (3) .... are fixed costs and variable costs combined. The solid line starting at point 0 shows the (4) .... at different levels of units sold. Point X is the (5) .... To the left of point X, the business is making a (6) .... To the right, the business is in (7) ....

21 If the price is right ...

In an interview with a journalist, Jan Horst, a marketing consultant, speaks about pricing policies. Complete the text of the interview with words or phrases from the box.

competition	discount	marginal cost	penetration strategy
cost plus	margin	market price	skimming strategy

Journalist: So, in terms of pricing, what mistakes do small companies often make?

Horst: They take the cost of sales, and add to it – inventing a (1) .... This is a (2) .... approach.

Journalist: What's the alternative?

Horst: First, fix a price somewhere near or below the competition, the (3) .... This can get you market share, using a so-called (4) ....

Journalist: What about (5) .... , just a bit above variable costs?

Horst: Marginal cost pricing only works if you have a lot of spare stock. It can help with a (6) .... policy.

Journalist: And how can pricing help to build up market share?

Horst: First, a low price is essential to build up market share in many markets. This is the penetration strategy approach. Or you can have a (7) .... , with high margins to help to pay costs quickly. This is often used with hi-tech goods. They start expensive but prices come down quickly once the (8) .... arrives.

22 Other aspects of profitability

Read the short text below on profitability. Match the underlined phrases (1–9) to phrases with a similar meaning in the box.

budgeted income statement	current liabilities	stock
capital employed	debtors	turnover
current assets	net income	work-in-progress

A *Assessing the strength of a company*

Two documents provide the necessary information for the most important decisions about the strength of a business: a (1) forecast profit and loss account and the present balance sheet.

B *Profitability*

A study of profitability must look at the relationship between:
- (2) income after all costs have been deducted and (3) total invoiced sales;
- net income and the amount of (4) money invested in the business.

C *Liquidity*

A study of a company's ability to make enough cash should show if:
- the planned cash balance is satisfactory;
- (5) people who owe money are likely to pay on time;
- (6) work which has been contracted but not yet invoiced or (7) finished goods will one day be sold;
- the relationship between fixed assets and (8) cash or other items of value which can easily be converted into cash is satisfactory;
- the relationship between current assets and (9) debts due for payment is satisfactory, i.e. current assets should be much greater than liabilities.

Management should be careful with forecasts, because budgeting is not a science and forecasts cannot be exact.

23 Key terms in measuring financial performance 1

The phrases on the left are commonly used in considerations of the financial strength of a company. Match each one to an appropriate explanation on the right. Use the grid below. (See example):

1 company accounts

2 profit and loss account

3 balance sheet

4 opening balance

5 closing balance

6 capital expenditure

7 fixed assets

8 current assets

9 net sales

10 pre-tax profit

11 interest paid

a) The description of income and expenditure in a specific accounting period.

b) Items of value which are not easily changed into cash but which the business needs.

c) Documents showing income, expenditure, assets and liabilities, sales records, etc.

d) Major spending on large items necessary for the business, such as property or equipment.

e) Cash items, or items that can easily be changed into cash for the present financial year.

f) The amount of money held in cash or near cash at the end of the accounting period.

g) The cost of borrowing from a bank.

h) Money made by the company, less all costs, but before tax has been paid.

i) The amount of money held in cash or near cash at the start of the accounting period.

j) The overall picture of assets and liabilities.

k) The profit from sales after direct costs have been deducted.

1	2	3	4	5	6	7	8	9	10	11
C										

24 Key terms in measuring financial performance 2

Change the <u>underlined</u> words or phrases in the sentences below to other words or phrases that have a similar meaning. Choose from the box.

abbreviated accounts	equity	liquid assets
capital investment	extraordinary items	operating income
consolidated	gross	revenue
debts		

1 <u>Unpredictable and exceptional costs</u> should be a separate item in the financial report.

2 The <u>trading income</u> needs to increase each year so that the company can make <u>decisions to buy new plant and equipment</u>.

3 The company accounts have been <u>checked and approved by an independent financial expert</u>.

4 Shareholders expect to see the <u>short description of the company's financial position</u>.

5 <u>Income</u> during the present tax year is less than last year.

6 <u>Pre-tax</u> earnings are down.

7 The <u>total value</u> of a company once all <u>liabilities</u> have been paid.

8 A successful company needs <u>property and investments that can be easily converted into cash</u>.

25 The balance sheet

Match the words or phrases on the left with the correct defintion (a–i). Use the grid below. (See example):

1 intangible assets

2 fixed assets

3 liquidity

4 depreciation

5 current assets

6 dividend

7 liabilities

8 liquid assets

9 overdraft

a) The money paid to shareholders out of profits.

b) Regular costs and money owed.

c) Any investments, cheques, bank deposits, stock or work-in-progress that can easily be converted into cash.

d) Assets which can be used to make immediate payments.

e) Property, land and equipment which is not normally intended for immediate sale.

f) Brand names, patents, rights, trade marks and licences which may be the major part of a company's wealth.

g) The total amount borrowed from a bank.

h) The ability of a company to pay suppliers, employees, shareholders, tax authorities, etc.

i) The notional fall in value of equipment over time.

1	2	3	4	5	6	7	8	9
f								

26 Reading a balance sheet

Look at this example of a balance sheet. Replace the <u>underlined</u> words or phrases with a word or phrase from the box with a similar meaning.

bank overdraft	land	preference shares	tax
capital reserves	ordinary shares	share capital	working capital
creditors	plant	stock	

BOGUS INDUSTRIES plc
Balance sheet as at 31 December 19..

	$000
ASSETS	
Fixed assets	
<u>(1) Property</u>	420
Buildings	180
<u>(2) Equipment</u> and machinery	100
Total fixed assets	**700**
Current assets	
Raw materials } <u>(3) goods</u>	
Work-in-progress } <u>held in</u>	200
Finished goods } <u>storage</u>	
Debtors	90
Cash in bank	60
Total current assets	**350**
Current liabilities	
<u>(4) People owed money</u>	80
<u>(5) Money owed to the bank</u>	50
<u>(6) Money owed to the government</u>	35
Total current liabilities	**165**
<u>**(7) Net current assets**</u>	**185**
Net assets	**885**
CAPITAL	
<u>(8) Money invested in the company and represented by shares</u>	
<u>(9) Shares paying a variable dividend to shareholders</u>	500
<u>(10) Shares paying a fixed dividend to shareholders</u>	300
<u>(11) Shares held in a special fund used to pay off creditors if the company goes into liquidation</u>	85
Total	**885**

27 Reading a profit and loss account

Fill in the missing words (1–7). Choose from the following:

cost of sales	expenses	overheads	sales income
depreciation	gross profit margin	pre-tax profit	

RBH plc

PROFIT AND LOSS ACCOUNT
for the year ending 31 December 19..

£000

(1)		2,450
(2)		
Materials	870	
Labour	790	
		1,660
(3) .... (profit)		
(4)		790
Salaries	220	
Capital expenditure	120	
Distribution	140	
Advertising	85	
Administration	80	
Bank loans, interest payments	38	
(5)		
Rent	12	
Heat, light, telephone	11	
Miscellaneous	8	
(6)	55	
		769
(7)		21

Note: *Depreciation* shows loss of value in capital equipment. It is not a real cash expenditure, but is usually shown this way in profit and loss accounts.

28 Introducing key terms in banking

Complete the words below to match the given meanings.

1 The person to whom a cheque is written.

p _ _ e _

2 Money provided by a bank to a customer,
for an agreed purpose.

l _ _ _

3 A bank which offers a full range of services to
individuals and companies.

c _ m _ _ _ _ _ _ l b _ _ _

4 A type of bank with a strong local or regional
identity, mainly used by small, private investors,
who get interest on their deposits.

s _ _ _ _ _ _   b _ _ _

5 An instruction from one bank to another bank
asking it to make a payment to a supplier.

_ _ _ k d _ _ _ _

6 An agreement that an account can remain in debit
up to a certain amount for an agreed time period.

o _ _ _ _ _ _ _ _

7 The time taken from when a cheque is presented
to a bank to when the receiving account is credited.

c _ _ _ r _ _ _ e

8 Fees charged by a bank for services provided.

_ _ n _ c _ _ _ _ _ s

9 An instruction from a customer to a bank to make a
regular payment to a creditor. Instructions to alter the
dates or the payments must come from the customer.

s _ _ _ _ _ _ g o _ _ _ r

10 A computer printout sent by a bank to a customer,
showing recent activity on his/her account.

s _ _ _ _ _ _ _ t

11 The lowest level of interest that a bank charges
for lending money.

b _ _ _ r _ _ _

29 Banking and using money

Label the pictures below using words from the box.

bank draft	.....
debit card	.....
bank statement	.....
paying-in slip	......
cash point	.....
teller	.....
cheque book	.....
withdrawal receipt	.....
night safe	.....

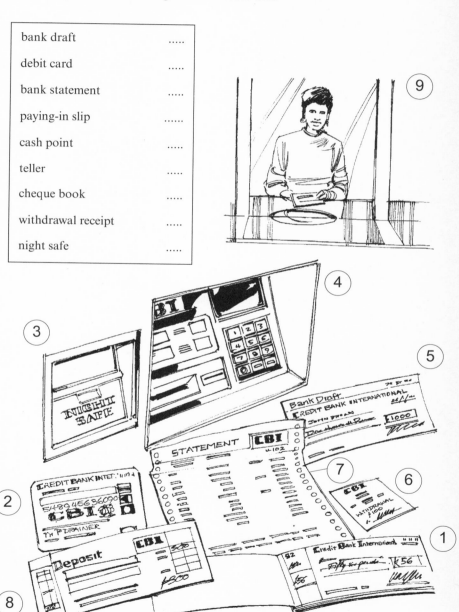

30 Banking services

A Credit Bank International offers the following services to customers planning
to export to new markets. Divide the products into two categories: **Finance**
and **Services**.

---

allowances against bills for collection

banker's order

bank transfer

buyer credit

economic information

foreign currency account

foreign currency loans and overdrafts

letter of credit

standing order

status enquiries

trade development advice

Finance

....

....

....

....

....

Services

....

....

....

....

....

....

B Look at the following extracts from a flyer for Credit Bank International. Complete the spaces using appropriate services or products from the box in **A** on the previous page.

CBI can help you develop an international business

Trading internationally

1 Our .... service offers an up-to-date assessment of the political and economic prospects in particular countries or regions.
2 We also provide .... which matches your company to a specific partner, either a customer or a supplier.
3 To make sure that your partner is reliable, we carry out .... , a check on their credit rating, to see if they have a good level of liquidity.
4 We offer finance to help your cashflow situation, using .... This means we provide a loan, and the money you are owed by a customer is a kind of security.
5 Or we lend money to your customer at fixed interest rates, so you get paid quickly. This is called ....

Foreign money

6 We also provide cash when you need it. We can set up .... This is good if you travel abroad a lot. This can be at fixed interest rates, so that you have no problems with changes in currency rates.
7 We can also provide a .... , with cheque books, overdraft facilities, bank cards and cash whenever you need them, in the foreign currency.

Paying your supplier

8 The easy and safe way to pay a supplier abroad is through a .... , though there are charges.
9 For regular business, payments can be made using a .... This is an agreement where the buyer can draw on amounts up to an agreed limit for an agreed purpose. The buyer sends all the relevant documents to the supplier. The supplier then takes the documents to a local bank to get paid.
10 Another way to make regular payments is using a .... , which pays a regular amount that can only be changed if you tell the bank to change it.
11 The alternative, useful if the amount changes regularly, is a .... , where the creditor can change the amount paid, or the dates for payment.

---

31 Bank charges

Choose the best explanation for each of the terms in *italics* from *a, b* or *c*.

1 *unauthorized overdraft fee*
a) a charge on an account if it goes into debit without an agreement from the bank
b) a charge on an account if it remains in credit after an overdraft agreement has been made
c) money paid into the bank to stop the account going into debit

2 *setting-up fee*
a) a charge made for a new account
b) a charge when money is paid in or taken out from an account
c) a fixed charge when an overdraft agreement is made

3 *base rates*
a) the rate of interest charged to customers who borrow from the bank
b) a rate used to help decide the level of interest on loans from the bank. (The bank usually sets the actual interest rate several points above the base rate.)
c) all charges made to an account in a year

4 *margin*
a) the percentage above the base rate that a borrower is asked to pay
b) the profit that a customer makes from having an account in credit and so earning interest
c) the cost of borrowing

5 *fixed rate lending*
a) an agreement to lend money at a current rate of interest that could change if base rates go up or down
b) lending money at an agreed interest rate for a fixed time
c) any agreement to lend money for a fixed period of time

6 *unauthorized overdraft fee*
a) a special low rate of interest charged to customers who are in difficulty
b) a higher rate of interest charged if an account is overdrawn above an agreed maximum
c) a single penalty fee charged to an account if it is overdrawn above an agreed maximum

7 *commission*
a) a percentage of a credit or debit which may be deducted by the bank
b) a request by a bank that more money should be paid into an account
c) a bonus paid by the bank to a customer if charges have been too high

8 *handling charge*
a) a special fee charged after a meeting with a customer
b) a fee charged by the bank in relation to a particular payment
c) a fee charged to an account for changing money from one currency to another

32 **Planning borrowing**

Organize the following into categories under the given headings, each of which would
be discussed with the bank in negotiating support for a business venture. (Four are
done for you as examples.)

---

experience   *financial projections*

capital needs   *assets*

purpose of borrowing   realism of financial projections

skills   insurance

track record   amount requested

ability to pay   business plan

existing capital resources   marketing plan

security   repayment method

Planning
financial projections

Requirements
capital needs

Business background
experience

Human resources

Protection of loan

Financial strength
assets

Repayment

33 Introducing key terms in insurance

Complete the words below to match the given meanings.

1 Payment made by an insurer.

i _ d _ _ _ _ _ y

2 A document which is evidence that someone has insurance.

i _ _ _ _ _ _ _ e c _ _ _ _ _ _ c _ _ _

3 Covered by insurance policy.

i _ _ _ _ _ d

4 Possibility that something might happen.

r _ _ _

5 The amount charged for insurance.

p _ _ _ _ _ m

6 Payment to help someone who has suffered loss or injury.

c _ _ p _ _ s _ _ _ _ _

7 Insurance protection.

c _ _ _ _

8 A small part of the total loss which should be paid by the insured person when he/she makes an insurance claim.

e _ _ _ _ s

9 A type of insurance which pays out on the death of the insured, or at a specific pre-determined time.

l _ _ _ a _ _ _ _ _ n _ _

10 A type of insurance to meet hospital costs after an accident or injury.

m _ _ _ _ _ l i _ _ _ _ _ _ _ e

11 A person whose job is to find appropriate insurance at an appropriate price.

b _ _ _ _ _

12 A description of what happened and a
   request to an insurer to meet the costs
   resulting from the event.   _ _ _ _ m

13 Someone other than the insured who
   suffers loss or injury in an accident.   t _ _ _ _ p _ _ _ _

14 A document issued by an insurance
   company describing the type of insurance
   offered and requesting payment.   s _ _ _ _ _ _ e

15 A document describing an insurance
   agreement.   p _ _ _ _ y

16 The period for which an insurance policy
   is effective.   t _ _ _

34 An insurance claim

Antonio Alessandro has sent a claim form to his insurer after a fire at his restaurant. He receives the reply below. Complete the text with appropriate words from the box.

claim	cover	legal costs	policy
compensation	estimate	loss adjuster	premium
comprehensive	indemnity	no claims bonus	

Bridge Insurance Ltd
124 Kew Gardens Road, London SW2 5HB
Tel: 0171 433 8211–15 Fax: 0171 433 563318

```
Antonio Alessandro
Ristorante Colosseo
120 Riverside Road
London EC23 5TR
2 March 19..

Dear Mr Alessandro
```
Re: Policy number DR 239981 R, Claim Ref. DR4381

Thank you for your (1) .... relating to the fire at your restaurant. We confirm that your policy is (2) .... and therefore covers fire.

Our (3) .... , Peter Carrow, will visit you on 7 March to see the damage.

You will receive (4) .... for all damage to the building and equipment. You should supply an (5) .... from two firms for the repairs. You will also receive (6) .... for loss of business, though you will have to make a separate claim. In addition, your (7) .... also provides (8) .... for any (9) .... which may arise.

Finally, we would like to inform you that your (10) .... will rise by 10% as your (11) .... will be affected by this incident.

```
Yours sincerely

Janina Piontek

Janina Piontek
Claims Manager
```

35 Key terms in investment

Find 10 key words or phrases concerned with investments which are hidden in the word square below.

R	D	P	S	H	A	R	E	S	O
E	I	N	T	E	R	E	S	T	M
T	V	F	R	T	E	G	L	O	G
U	I	N	N	I	L	Z	O	C	R
R	D	F	B	A	C	B	S	K	O
N	E	A	R	N	I	N	G	S	W
I	N	V	E	S	T	M	E	N	T
T	D	N	D	L	X	P	O	T	H
F	E	B	F	U	T	U	R	E	S
P	O	R	T	F	O	L	I	O	R

36 Describing trends 2

Rewrite the following sentences, beginning with the given words, and replacing the words in *italics* with a verb phrase. (See example):

1 There has been a *marked rise* in sales for Axal in recent weeks.
   Axal sales ...

   Axal sales have risen markedly in recent weeks.

2 Frodo has suffered *a sudden drop* in market share.
   Frodo's market share ...

3 Spino showed *a slight fall* in share price last week.
   Spino's share price ...

4 There will be *a quick recovery* in the share price.
   The share price will ...

5 *A levelling off* of sales for FDT is expected.
   FDT sales ...

6 There has been *a considerable decline* in the market.
   The market ...

7 There was *a sharp increase* in share prices.
   Share prices ...

8 *The wild fluctuation* in share values was because of the price war.
   Share prices ...

9 HD experienced *a rapid climb* in market share in the early 1990s.
   HD's market share ...

37 Describing share movements

Match each of the following phrases to an appropriate graph below showing recent share performance. Look at the line between the two crosses.

collapsed
fell back
rallied
stepped out
edged down
firmed
steadied

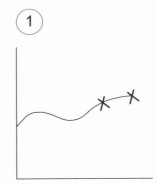

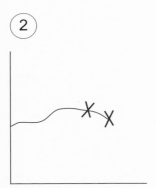

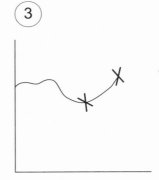

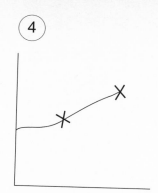

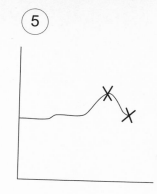

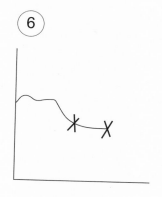

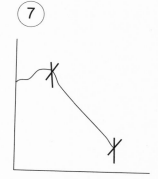

38 Stock Exchanges

Complete the crossword below.

Across

1 The city which is the financial capital of Germany. (9)

5 Goods like coffee, tea, cocoa, metals and oil that are traded in large quantities. (11)

6 The index of share prices in the New York Stock Exchange. (3, 5)

7 An acronym for a company that has shares quoted on the UK Stock Exchange. (3)

9 A computer measurement of the share performance of 100 leading UK companies. (7)

10 A contract to buy shares at a fixed price in the future. (6)

11 A part of a company's total capital that can be bought and sold. (5)

Down

2 A method of raising capital by selling new shares to existing shareholders at a low price. (6, 5)

3 Safe investments in the largest and most powerful companies. (4, 4)

4 A relatively safe investment issued by governments or large companies which earns interest for the holder. (4)

8 The place where stocks and shares are traded in Paris. (6)

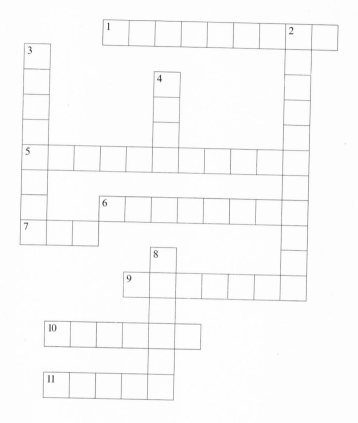

39 Market reports

The words in *italics* in the following sentences are commonly used to describe share movements. Divide them into three columns: **Up**, **Down**, **Same**.

1 Burlesque shares *peaked* at 450p.

2 After steady rises, Axam shares *levelled off* at 320p.

3 Harrow *ended higher*, up 10p.

4 AJL *fell back* 20p.

5 Roadman *added* 5p in busy trading.

6 Media shares *sank* on news of planned government regulation.

7 News Newspaper Group *dipped* 20p to 540.

8 By the close of trading, Hamley *steadied* at 320p.

9 Most of the oil sector *improved* in a bullish market.

10 Dolman *ended lower* at 320, off 20p.

11 Following steady gains, Koman Foods *firmed* at 196p.

12 Food companies were generally up, *gaining* on the back of improved retail forecasts.

13 Bearish output forecasts indicate *sliding* share prices in the coming weeks.

Up	Down	Same
....	....	....
....	....	....
....	....	....
....	....	....
....	....	....
....	....	

40 Managing a personal investment portfolio

Match the term on the left with an appropriate definition on the right (a–l).
Use the grid below. (See example):

1 consultant
2 insurance
3 investment
4 investment broker
5 investor
6 pension
7 priority
8 portfolio
9 risk
10 sector
11 stake
12 term insurance

a) Someone who buys and sells stocks and shares or other types of investment, such as life assurance policies, insurance, etc.

b) The most important thing.

c) An area of the economy, e.g. oil, pharmaceuticals, electrodomestic goods.

d) How safe an investment is.

e) A part ownership in a company, usually by having shares in it.

f) A kind of life assurance for a specific time period.

g) Any attempt to spend money so that you have more money in the future.

h) A regular amount of money that you get when you stop working because of your age.

i) The total collection of investments that an individual has.

j) A specialist who offers advice.

k) A type of investment which provides protection against accidents.

l) Someone who invests their money, usually in private companies.

1	2	3	4	5	6	7	8	9	10	11	12
j											

41 **Mutual funds**

Complete the following sentences with words or phrases from the box.

invested	investment trusts	mutual funds	OEICS	redeemed
trade	traded	transaction	trust law	unit trusts

1 .... are companies set up to invest capital for investors.

2 .... are a type of mutual fund common in the UK and English-speaking countries. They are a safe, easy investment.

3 .... is the legal framework which governs the management of private trusts.

4 Unit trust investments are easily .... or turned into cash.

5 When capital is .... in unit trusts, more shares are created.

6 .... have a share base which is constant – new investments buy existing shares, they do not create new shares.

7 Both mutual trusts and investment trusts have low .... costs, which means buying into or selling out is not expensive.

8 .... are open-ended investment vehicles

9 OEICS are flexible and easy to .... , having a single price for both selling and buying.

10 OEICS are .... internationally.

42 Planning for the future

A Match the type of investment on the left with the correct description on the right (a–d)

1 Occupational Pension Plan

    a) • pension scheme for employees
       • flexible, easily moved; so good for people who
       • may change jobs frequently
       • the employee takes the plan to the new employer

2 Personal Equity Plan

    b) • extremely safe investment
       • tax free interest
       • operated by banks and building societies
       • limited annual investment

3 Individual Savings Account

    c) • tax advantages (e.g. tax free dividends)
       • the money is invested on world stock exchanges
       • growth depends on the performance of stocks
       • there is risk if the investments are in companies which perform badly

4 Group Pension Plan

    d) • run by companies investing part of their own money and part of the employee's salary
       • linked to a person's final salary on retirement
       • pensions can be increased by making additional voluntary contributions (AVCs)

B Mark the following statements as True or False. If they are false, explain why.

	True	False
1 ISA is a common acronym for Individual Savings Account.	☐	☐
2 PEP is a common acronym for Personal Equity Plan.	☐	☐
3 Addittional Voluntary Contributions means you have to pay extra into the fund.	☐	☐
4 Retirement is when you stop working.	☐	☐
5 A short-term investment is when you plan to invest the money for many years.	☐	☐
6 Tax exempt means you have to pay tax on profits from the investment.	☐	☐
7 A reasonably safe investment means low risk.	☐	☐
8 Linked to final salary means the same salary as on retirement.	☐	☐
9 Occupational Pension Plans are paid for by employees and employers.	☐	☐
10 Personal Equity Plans are based on investments in the world markets.	☐	☐

43 Key words in talking about company relationships

Match each of the words or phrases on the left to an appropriate definition (a–l). Use the grid below. (See example):

1 bid
2 buyout
3 competitor
4 divestiture
5 flotation
6 joint venture
7 merger
8 parent company
9 stake
10 sister company
11 stock
12 takeover

a) A proportion of the total share capital of a company.

b) Buying a majority of the shares in a company, and so winning control over the company.

c) Joining together of the stock of two companies, so they become part of the same company.

d) The total equity capital of a company, held by shareholders in the form of shares.

e) An offer to buy part of the share capital of a company.

f) A company which owns more than 50% of the shares in another company.

g) The relationship between two companies, both owned by the same parent company.

h) Selling equity capital in a company, and so ending ownership of the company.

i) A situation where workers or management buy all the equity (or more than 50%), or buy other assets, and so gain control of a business.

j) A business which is trying to sell in the same market as another business.

k) The open sale to private investors of shares in a company on the Stock Exchange.

l) A temporary arrangement where two companies work together for a particular project.

1	2	3	4	5	6	7	8	9	10	11	12
e											

44 Competitive tendering and joint bids

Read the following definitions and match them to words in **bold** in the advertisement below. (See example):

1 A group of companies who work together only for a particular contract.

   Consortium

2 A company owned and run by two or more people who do not receive interest on capital invested in the company.

   ....

3 A company which is 100% owned by a parent company.

   ....

4 A project with two or more partners.

   ....

5 Someone brought in to work on part of a large project.

   ....

6 A formal proposal to do something at a certain price in a certain time period.

   ....

Puertos Secos S.A.

CALL FOR BIDS

Puertos Secos S.A. (the sponsor) invite offers for the operation of a dry port facility at Barajas, Madrid.

Tenders will be accepted from any **partnership**, private company, or **consortium**, including companies operating with **wholly-owned subsidiaries**, or partially-owned subsidiaries, or other **joint-venture agreements**. The use of **sub-contractors** is acceptable.

However the contract will be awarded to a single individual or company who shall be responsible for the management of the project.

Details from:
Ministerio de Asuntos Interiores, Departamento de Trasportes,
c/Bernardino Obregón, 44–48, 28012 MADRID. Tel: (9) 1 530 09 06

---

45 Company strength and market position

Complete the words below to match the given meanings.

1 To grow, to get bigger .   _ x _ _ _ d

2 To stop activities that do not make much money
   and to reduce the number of staff .   r _ t _ _ _ _ l _ _ _

3 The action of winning ownership and control of
   another company.   _ _ q _ _ _ _ _ _ _ n

4 To join two companies to create one bigger company.   _ m _ _ g _ _ _ t _

5 A company that is owned by a parent company.   s _ _ s _ _ _ _ _ _

6 One company taking control of another, smaller one.   t _ _ _ o _ _ _

7 Where one company is the only supplier to a
   particular market.   m _ _ _ p _ _ _

8 Where a parent company sells a subsidiary
   (the opposite of number 3 above).   d _ v _ _ _ _ t _ _ _

9 A large group, owning and controlling
   many companies .   h _ _ _ _ _ g c _ _ _ _ _

10 An illegal agreement between two or more
    companies to fix high prices.   c _ _ t _ _

11 Fixing low prices until a competitor goes
    out of business.   p _ _ _ _ w _ _

12 Two companies joining together to create
    one company.   m _ _ _ _ _

13 A demerger, two companies separate.   b _ _ _ _ u _

46 Miscellaneous word phrases

The words in this test relate to different aspects of trading and investment in an international business environment. Complete the phrases with an appropriate word from the box below.

black	bonus	break	bridging	intangible	interim	issue
line	loss	red	reserves	retail	securities	

1 The part of an economy which is not declared to the tax authorities is known as the .... *economy.*

2 A business that is losing money is *running at a* ....

3 A bank account that is in deficit is *in the* ....

4 Free shares given to long-term shareholders are called .... *shares.*

5 If a business will meet its costs but not make any profit, it will .... *even.*

6 If you want to buy something quickly you can borrow money on your assets by taking out a .... *loan.* You pay back the loan after you sell some assets.

7 The final return on a business deal, indicating whether the deal made a profit or not, is sometimes called *the bottom* ....

8 A measure of prices paid in the shops is the .... *price index.*

9 The payment to shareholders at the half-year point is called the .... *dividend.*

10 The price of shares when a company is first floated on the Stock Exchange is called the .... *price.*

11 Large amounts of foreign currency held by a company, bank or government, as a security against changes in exchange rates, is called *foreign currency* ....

12 Stocks and shares held by governments are called *government* ....

13 Assets which have a value but cannot be seen, e.g. customer goodwill, patents or trade marks, are called .... *assets.*

47 Deregulating markets and bringing in competition

A The words below are all related to the theme of industrial sectors and international competition. Complete the table with the correct form of the given words.

Verb	Personal noun	General noun	Adjective
	m	monopoly	
	competitor		
deregulate	–		
	–		authorized
	legislator		
		protection	
nationalize	–		
	regulator		
		partnership	–
	trader		traded/trading
	–		subsidized

B Use appropriate forms of the words on the previous page to complete the text below. It is part of a newspaper report on changes in the European telecommunications industry.

BT TO GAIN FROM EU COMPETITION LAWS

British Telecom is going to attack the (1) ....
position of its German (2) .... , Deutsche
Telekom. BT wants a (3) .... with two
German competitors, RWE and Viag. The EU is trying to
(4) .... the European telecoms industry.
The EU wants to increase competition and open up
(5) .... across frontiers. In France,
for example, France Telecom is in a strongly
(6) .... domestic market. The company is
also (7) .... by the government.

48 Financing problems

The text below is about companies in difficulty. First read the short text, then choose the best explanation for each term given below.

Sam Air Grounded

Sam Air is going to call in the receivers. The aircraft company does not have a serious bidder, after inviting partners to join a restructuring plan.

Sam Air's major creditor, Credit Bank International, refused to reschedule payments and has called in the debt. The company will probably go into liquidation soon. A rights issue failed three years ago when shareholders refused to put in more capital.

---

1 *receivers*

  a) directors of a company

  b) accountants who close down a company and give its assets to creditors and shareholders

  c) shareholders who receive the assets of a company that stops trading

2 *restructuring*

  a) reorganization of how the company is run

  b) reducing company costs by cutting the work-force

  c) reorganizing the ownership of equity capital and the way debts are financed

3 *to reschedule payments*

    a) to increase the amount of interest

    b) to change the terms for paying back a loan

    c) to ask for a loan to be taken over by another lender

4 *to call in a debt*

    a) to ask a creditor to pay what is owed

    b) to increase interest payments on a debt

    c) to agree to late payment of a debt

5 *go into liquidation*

    a) stop trading and have all assets given to creditors and shareholders

    b) be declared bankrupt

    c) change the type of activity of the business

6 *rights issue*

    a) an attempt to enter new markets

    b) an attempt to change the company into a workers' co-operative

    c) a way of getting extra money into a company by selling shares to existing shareholders at a low price.

49 Understanding news stories

Below are headings from newspaper reports on the business environment. Choose the best explanation of the keywords from *a*, *b*, or *c*.

Growth in America lowest since 1990

1 Growth means ...
   a) increased gross domestic product (GDP), or the increase in total sales revenue
   b) improved exports for the US economy
   c) increased value of companies on the New York Stock Exchange

Consumer confidence down in Germany

2 Consumer confidence means ...
   a) what people think about German industry
   b) what people think of their personal economic situation
   c) what shop owners think of business prospects

Japan's trade surplus falls

3 Trade surplus means ...
   a) the positive balance in exports over imports
   b) the value of sales
   c) the share value of the top 100 Japanese companies

Tokai bank writes off Yen 8bn in bad debts

4 To write off debts means ...
   a) get the money back from creditors
   b) forget the money, since the loans are not going to be paid back
   c) demand the money back immediately

Cleveland Best Inc. announces demerger

5 A demerger is ...
   a) a return to two separate entities following a period as one company
   b) a decision to split a company into two parts
   c) a temporary division

Ireland's trade deficit with Germany smaller

6 A trade deficit is ...
   a) where exports are larger than imports

b) a positive balance in favour of sales over debts

c) where the value of imports is greater than the value of exports

Oil industry confidence hit by overcapacity and oil price slump

7 Overcapacity means ...

a) the industry is not producing enough to meet demand

b) production facilities are not working to their potential

c) supply is greater than demand

Italian chemical conglomerate to break up

8 A conglomerate is ...

a) a large manufacturing company

b) a multinational company

c) a large holding company with many subsidiaries

Worldwide PC sales soar 70%

9 To soar means ...

a) increase by a large amount

b) go up a little

c) fall dramatically

Corporate phone bills to fall

10 Corporate means ...

a) large

b) big business

c) personal, domestic and business

Worldwide corporate tax hits 40%

11 Corporate tax means ...

a) special rate of tax on companies with large turnovers

b) taxes on any business activity

c) taxes on everyone, private individuals and companies

James Inc. makes $2bn from home entertainments sell-off

12 A sell-off is ...

a) a successful sales campaign

b) a special promotion of low price goods

c) a decision to sell a subsidiary in an industrial group

50 Key economic terms

Match the words on the left with the correct definition (a–l). Use the grid below. (See example):

1 central bank

2 exchange rate

3 inflation

4 interest rates

5 invisible earnings

6 manufacturing industry

7 national debt

8 public sector borrowing requirement

9 public spending

10 service sector

11 training

12 unemployment rate

a) Education and skills development for young people and the unemployed.

b) The part of the economy that does not make goods. Also known as the tertiary sector.

c) The money a government needs to borrow to pay for what it does.

d) The value of a national currency against other currencies.

e) The annual cost of borrowing money from a bank.

f) A measure of retail price increases.

g) The principal national banking authority.

h) The part of the economy that makes products and changes raw materials into products.

i) The number, or percentage, of people out of work.

j) Government spending.

k) The total amount of money that a government owes.

l) Income in foreign currency for services such as banking, insurance, tourism.

1	2	3	4	5	6	7	8	9	10	11	12
g											

51 Acronyms and abbreviations

Complete what the following stand for:

1 IMF   I _ _ _ _ _ _ _ _ _ _ _ Monetary F _ _ _

2 OPEC   O _ _ _ _ _ _ _ _ _ _ of Petroleum E _ _ _ _ _ _ _ Countries

3 PSBR   P _ _ _ _ _ S _ _ _ _ _ Borrowing Requirement

4 GATT   General A _ _ _ _ _ _ _ _ on Tariffs and T _ _ _ _

5 EU   E _ _ _ _ _ _ _ U _ _ _ _

6 GNP   Gross N _ _ _ _ _ _ _ P _ _ _ _ _ _

7 OECD   O _ _ _ _ _ _ _ _ _ _ _ for E _ _ _ _ _ _ _
Co-operation and Development

8 ASEAN   A _ _ _ _ _ _ _ _ _ _ of South East A _ _ _ _ N _ _ _ _ _ _

9 IBRD   International B _ _ _ for Reconstruction and
D _ _ _ _ _ _ _ _ _ _

10 WWF   World W _ _ _ _ _ _ _ Fund

11 UN   U _ _ _ _ _ N _ _ _ _ _ _

12 WHO   W _ _ _ _ Health O _ _ _ _ _ _ _ _ _ _ _

52 Economic indicators

Mark the following sentences as True or False. If they are false, explain why.

	True	False
1 Inflation is a measure of increasing prices.	❏	❏
2 High inflation generally means increasing unemployment.	❏	❏
3 A healthy consumer economy always means lower unemployment.	❏	❏
4 Higher investment in training and education is easier during a low point in the economic cycle.	❏	❏
5 A tight fiscal policy means high taxation and high government spending.	❏	❏
6 Governments need to control their borrowing requirement.	❏	❏
7 A high value of the local currency is good for exports.	❏	❏
8 Housebuilding is seen as a good indicator of what is happening in the domestic economy.	❏	❏
9 Gross national product (GNP) is a measure of the annual value of sales of goods and services in a country, and it does not include sales for companies abroad.	❏	❏
10 Capacity utilization is a measure of how many people are in work.	❏	❏
11 Generally, high levels of supply and low levels of demand means unemployment falls.	❏	❏
12 Growth creates wealth and wealth creates jobs.	❏	❏

	True	**False**
13 Rationalization means cutting labour costs so people lose their jobs.	❏	❏
14 Increased investment in real terms means increased investment above inflation rates.	❏	❏
15 A balance of payments deficit means a company is spending more than it earns.	❏	❏

53 Managing the economy

Here are six newspaper headlines. Below them are the first lines of six articles. Match the headline to the right article.

1 **Retail sales up – good news for jobs**

2 **Call for investment in training**

3 *Reflation would help housebuilding, says top official*

4 *Inflation target still 3%*

5 **Higher taxes destroy potential for growth**

6 *Call for devaluation*

a) The Prime Minister has said again that retail prices must not rise above present levels. Speaking at a party meeting, he said low inflation was essential for economic recovery.

b) An industrial pressure group has reported that the strength of the pound is damaging exports. The National Association of Exporting Industries recommends that the Government should devalue the pound by 10–12%. Exports have fallen by 5% as the pound has risen against all major currencies ...

c) A report published this week claims that the increase in consumer spending is creating new employment opportunities.

d) The depressed construction industry would benefit if the Government increased public spending and lowered taxes, according to ...

e) The Government should spend more on training grants for young people and the unemployed, according to Jaqueline Ross, the region's Local Education Officer. This would bring long-term economic benefits ...

f) The Minister of State for Finance, Peter Bluff, said yesterday that tax increases would be bad for industry. 'The best industrialists would leave the country and the damage to the national economy could be massive,' Mr Bluff said.

54 Economic performance

The sentences below are extracts from a newspaper report on economic performance. Choose the correct explanation for the words in **bold** from *a*, *b*, or *c*.

1 **Retail sales** continued to grow in March, confirming the trend begun in the pre-Christmas boom, according to Paul Figg, of IMA Consultants.
   a) sales in the shops
   b) sales of clothes
   c) factory prices

2 Consumer demand will help **economic growth**, forecast at 4% for the year.
   a) price rises
   b) jobs
   c) total national income

3 Higher consumption of imported goods could result in a worsening **trade deficit**.
   a) decline in trade
   b) negative balance of value of exports and imports
   c) inflation

4 Uncertainty in the industrial job market is creating a lack of **consumer confidence**.
   a) employment in manufacturing
   b) spending in the shops
   c) feel-good factor in ordinary people

5 **Manufacturing output** is lower and exports have almost halved.
   a) building new factories
   b) industrial production
   c) employment in factories

6 There is a problem of excessive **stock levels** which means there are no new jobs.
   a) goods waiting to be sold
   b) strikes
   c) high prices

7 There is an economic slowdown in most major **export markets**.
   a) countries which normally export to this country.
   b) countries which normally buy from us.
   c) Stock Exchanges

55 Managing exchange rates

The sentences below describe how different economic factors affect each other.
Complete the spaces with words or phrases from the box.

balance of payments	deficit	interest rates
building societies	exchange rates	unemployment
consumer spending	exports	

When banks and (1) .... offer credit, or cheap loans at low
(2) .... , consumer spending rises and (3) .... go up.
High (4) .... creates pressure to increase wages.
High consumer spending also creates more demand for imports. This causes
problems for the (5) .... Imports also cost more when the
exchange rate is high.
A high exchange rate also means lower (6) ....
Together these factors can make a worse balance of payments
(7) .... and higher inflation.
Higher inflation usually leads to higher (8) ....

56 Central banks and economic stability

Choose the correct phrase from the alternatives in *italics* to create eight true sentences about economic management.

1 Most people think *politicians / bankers* are better than *politicians / bankers* at running an economy.

2 Independent central banks have a good record on controlling *inflation / public opinion*.

3 Freedom to control *monetary policy / banking regulations* means being able to change *exchange rates / political opinion*.

4 *Low interest rates / high interest rates* help to control *inflation / small banks*.

5 High interests rates often cause *small banks / central banks* to fail.

6 In developing countries, central banks cannot help small banks because of the risk of *low inflation / hyper-inflation*.

7 Newly independent central banks are limited by their agreements with *the International Monetary Fund / the United Nations*.

8 Any risk of inflation can mean *disinvestment / new investment* from *investment fundholders / national governments*.

57 Friedman is not dead and Keynes lives

Read the imaginary dialogue below. It is between two economists: Milton Friedman, who believes in leaving everything to market forces; and J.M. Keynes, who believes in partnership between the State and private capital. They are discussing the impact of the European Airbus project on the world airliner market. Fill in the spaces with appropriate words from the box.

competition	economies	market share	scale
competitor	export subsidies	monopoly	subsidies
consortium	free trade	resources	suppliers

Keynes: The Airbus project has been good for consumers. It has stopped Boeing having a (1) .... in the airliner market.

Friedman: In fact, Boeing already had a (2) .... in McDonnell Douglas.

Keynes: Yes, it did. But the Airbus did lower prices due to the arrival of more (3) ....

Friedman: But the benefits of Airbus do not match the subsidy which the European taxpayer paid for. (4) .... is the best way to run the global economy. It is cheaper than tariff barriers, import quotas and (5) ....

Keynes: I can't agree. The airliner industry has few companies. They can make (6) .... of (7) .... This means low costs and real competition between (8) .... This is what happened between Boeing and Airbus. The Airbus (9) .... , with four countries, has built up (10) .... The benefit to the European economy has been more than the cost of the (11) ....

Friedman: I am not sure. I think subsidies are a waste of (12) ....

Keynes: Well, I think I'll have a cup of tea. Will you join me?

Friedman: Only if it's free market tea.

Note:
Biographical details

Milton Friedman, economist, born New York, 1912– .

John Maynard Keynes, economist, born Cambridge, UK, 1883–1946.

Answers

ɔ

SECTION 1: INTRODUCING KEY TERMS IN FINANCE

Test 1

1 e)
2 h)
3 a)
4 j)
5 c)
6 d)
7 i)
8 b)
9 f)
10 g)

Test 2

1 m)
2 b)
3 a)
4 l)
5 k)
6 j)
7 h)
8 e)
9 f)
10 c)
11 n)
12 i)
13 o)
14 g)
15 d)

Test 3

	Verb	Personal noun	General noun	Adjective
1	to analyze	analyst	analysis	analytical
2	to compete	competitor	competition	competitive
3	to advise	advisor	advice	–
4	to merge	–	merger	merged
5	to industrialize	industrialist	industry	industrial
6	to trade	trader	trade	trading/ traded
7	to export	exporter	export(s)	exporting/exported
8	to produce	producer	product	productive
9	to supply	supplier	supply	supplied
10	to consume	consumer	consumption	consuming
11	to guarantee	guarantor	guarantee	guaranteed
12	to credit	creditor	credit	credited
13	to debit	debtor	debit	debited
14	to earn	earner	earnings	earned
15	to invest	investor	investment	invested

Test 4

table	1
row	2
column	3
pie chart	4
segment	5
histogram/bar graph	6
vertical axis	7
horizontal axis	8
line graph	9
dotted line	10
solid line	11
broken line	12
curve	13
fluctuating line	14
undulating line	15

Test 5

1 d)
2 e)
3 a)
4 b)
5 h)
6 g)
7 f)
8 i)
9 c)

Test 6

A

rise/fall
increase/decrease
go up/go down
climb/decline
shrink/expand
deteriorate/improve
get better/get worse
collapse/escalate
hit bottom/peak

B

stay the same	1
edge down	2
recover	3
collapse	4
reach a peak	5
increase steadily	6
decline to nothing	7
rise slightly	8
fluctuate	9

Test 7

	SINGLE INDIVIDUAL OWNS COMPANY	TWO OR MORE OWNERS/ DIRECTORS	QUOTED ON STOCK EXCHANGE	WORKERS RUN THE COMPANY	UNLIMITED LIABILITY	LIMITED LIABILITY	OWNER IS SELF-EMPLOYED
PUBLIC LIMITED COMPANY		✓	✓			✓	
PRIVATE LIMITED COMPANY	possibly	✓				✓	
SOLE TRADER	✓				✓		✓
PARTNERSHIP		✓			✓		possibly
CO-OPERATIVE				✓		possibly	

Test 8

1	VAT	Value Added Tax
2	PLC	Public Limited Company
3	Ltd	Limited
4	& Co.	and Company
5	CWO	Cash With Order
6	COD	Cash On Delivery
7	c.i.f.	cost, insurance, freight.
8	PAYE	Pay-As-You-Earn (i.e. tax)
9	p/e	price/earnings ratio
10	P & L account	Profit and Loss account

SECTION 2: FINANCIAL PLANNING

Test 9

1 profitability
2 turnover
3 core activity
4 gross profit margin
5 setting-up costs
6 overheads
7 net profit margin
8 cost of sales
9 break-even point
10 selling costs

Test 10

fixed costs
labour costs (2)
storage costs (7)
administrative costs (4)

variable costs
production costs (3)
advertising costs (1)
distribution costs (5)
selling costs (6)

Test 11

1 fixed costs
2 variable costs
3 manufacturing costs
4 selling costs
5 labour costs
6 operating costs

7 cost price
8 cost analysis
9 cost centre
10 cost of sales

Test 12

1 income
2 forecast
3 sheet
4 budget
5 turnover
6 fixed
7 variable
8 raw
9 capital
10 administrative
11 cash

Test 13

1 petty cash
2 hard cash
3 cashflow
4 cash on delivery
5 cash budget
6 cash advance
7 ready cash
8 cash settlement
9 cash price

Test 14

A
Report: 2, 1, 5, 4, 3

B
Memo: 4, 2, 5, 1, 3

Test 15

1 demand
2 margin
3 price-sensitive
4 passed its sell-by-date
5 price cut
6 inelastic
7 annual sales
8 turnover

SECTION 3: MANAGING COMPANY FINANCES

Test 16

A
1 b)
2 c)
3 d)
4 a)

B

1 d)
2 f)
3 g)
4 c)
5 h)
6 b)
7 e)
8 a)

Test 17

1 sales revenue
2 variable costs
3 total
4 variable
5 fixed
6 fixed costs
7 unit contribution

Test 18

Services
electricity account
telephone

Insurance
professional indemnity insurance
employer's liability insurance

Property
rent
mortgage payments

Vehicles
car and van hire
car hire purchase agreements

Employee costs
salaries
employee national insurance contributions

Administration
secretarial support

Equipment
equipment, machinery
leasing of computers

Professional fees
accountancy fees

Miscellaneous fixed costs
books, newspapers
stationery and printing

Test 19

1 a)
2 b)

3 c)
4 a)
5 b)
6 b)
7 c)
8 a)
9 b)
10 b)

Test 20

1 fixed costs
2 variable costs
3 total costs
4 sales revenue
5 break-even point
6 loss
7 profit

Test 21

1 margin
2 cost plus
3 market price
4 penetration strategy
5 marginal cost
6 discount
7 skimming strategy
8 competition

Test 22

1 budgeted income statement
2 net income
3 turnover
4 capital employed
5 debtors
6 work-in-progress
7 stock
8 current assets
9 current liabilities

SECTION 4: MEASURING FINANCIAL PERFORMANCE

Test 23

1 c)
2 a)
3 j)
4 i)
5 f)
6 d)
7 b)
8 e)
9 k)
10 h)
11 g)

Test 24

1 extraordinary items
2 operating income, capital investment
3 consolidated
4 abbreviated accounts
5 revenue
6 gross
7 equity, debts
8 liquid assets

Test 25

1 f)
2 e)
3 h)
4 i)
5 c)
6 a)
7 b)
8 d)
9 g)

Test 26

1 land
2 plant
3 stocks
4 creditors
5 bank overdraft
6 tax
7 working capital
8 share capital
9 ordinary shares
10 preference shares
11 capital reserves

Test 27

1 sales income
2 expenses
3 gross profit margin
4 cost of sales
5 overheads
6 depreciation
7 pre-tax profit

SECTION 5:
BANKING AND INSURANCE

Test 28

1 payee
2 loan
3 commercial bank
4 savings bank
5 bank draft
6 overdraft
7 clearance
8 bank charges

9 standing order
10 statement
11 base rate

Test 29

1 cheque book
2 debit card
3 night safe
4 cash point
5 bank draft
6 withdrawal receipt
7 bank statement
8 paying-in slip
9 teller

Test 30

A
Finance
allowances against bills for collection
buyer credit
foreign currency account
foreign currency loans and overdrafts
letter of credit

Services
bank transfer
banker's order
economic information
standing order
status enquiries
trade development advice

B

1 economic information (service)
2 trade development advice
3 status enquiries
4 allowances against bills for collection
5 buyer credit
6 foreign currency loans and overdrafts
7 foreign currency account
8 bank transfer
9 letter of credit
10 standing order
11 banker's order

Test 31

1 a)
2 c)
3 b)
4 a)
5 b)
6 c)
7 a)
8 b)

78

Test 32
Planning
financial projections
business plan
realism of financial projections

Requirements
capital needs
amount requested
purpose of borrowing

Business Background
experience
track record
marketing plan.

Human Resources
skills

Financial Strength
assets
security
existing capital resources

Protection of Loan
insurance

Repayment
repayment method
ability to pay

Test 33
1 indemnity
2 insurance certificate
3 insured
4 risk
5 premium
6 compensation
7 cover
8 excess
9 life assurance
10 medical insurance
11 broker
12 claim
13 third party
14 schedule
15 policy
16 term

Test 34
1 claim
2 comprehensive
3 loss adjuster
4 indemnity
5 estimate
6 compensation

7 policy
8 cover
9 legal costs
10 premium
11 no claims bonus

SECTION 6:
INVESTING YOUR MONEY

Test 35

R	D	P	S	H	A	R	E	S	O
E	I	N	T	E	R	E	S	T	M
T	V	F	R	T	E	G	L	O	G
U	I	N	N	I	L	Z	O	C	R
R	D	F	B	A	C	B	S	K	O
N	E	A	R	N	I	N	G	S	W
I	N	V	E	S	T	M	E	N	T
T	D	N	D	L	X	P	O	T	H
F	E	B	F	U	T	U	R	E	S
P	O	R	T	F	O	L	I	O	R

Test 36
1 Axal sales have risen markedly in recent weeks
2 Frodo's market share has dropped suddenly.
3 Spino's share price fell slightly last week.
4 The share price will recover quickly.
5 FDT sales will/should level off.
6 The market has declined considerably.
7 Share prices increased sharply.
8 Share prices fluctuated wildly because of the price war.
9 HD's market share climbed rapidly in the early 1990s.

Test 37
1 firmed
2 edged down
3 rallied
4 stepped out
5 fell back
6 steadied
7 collapsed

Test 38
Across
1 Frankfurt
5 commodities
6 Dow Jones

7 PLC
9 Footsie
10 Future
11 Share

Down

2 rights issue
3 blue chip
4 bond
8 Bourse

Test 39
Up
peaked
ended higher
added
improved
firmed
gaining

Down
fell back
sank
dipped
ended lower
sliding

Same
levelled off
steadied

Test 40
1 j)
2 k)
3 g)
4 a)
5 l)
6 h)
7 b)
8 i)
9 d)
10 c)
11 e)
12 f)

Test 41
1 mutual funds
2 unit trusts
3 trust law
4 redeemed
5 invested
6 investment trusts
7 transaction
8 OEICS
9 trade
10 traded

Test 42
A
1 d)
2 c)
3 b)
4 a)

B
1 True
2 True
3 False. Voluntary means optional.
4 True
5 False. Short-term investment means only a short time.
6 False. Tax exempt means you pay no tax on profits from the investment.
7 True
8 False. Linked to final salary means *a proportion of* the final salary.
9 True
10 True

SECTION 7: COMPANIES AND
THE BUSINESS ENVIRONMENT

Test 43
1 3)
2 i)
3 j)
4 h)
5 k)
6 l)
7 c)
8 f)
9 a)
10 g)
11 d)
12 b)

Note: A merger is usually regarded positively by both parties involved. Both may be large companies, perhaps operating in slightly different but complimentary markets. A takeover is often seen as a negative development by the smaller party.

Test 44
1 consortium
2 partnership
3 wholly-owned subsidiary
4 joint-venture agreement
5 sub-contractor
6 tender

Test 45
1 expand
2 rationalize

3 acquisition
4 amalgamate
5 subsidiary
6 takeover
7 monopoly
8 divestiture
9 holding company
10 cartel
11 price war
12 merger
13 break up

Test 46

1 black economy
2 running at a loss
3 in the red
4 bonus shares
5 break even
6 bridging loan
7 the bottom line
8 retail price index (also known as *consumer price index* in US)
9 interim dividend
10 issue price
11 foreign currency reserves
12 government securities
13 intangible assets (also known as *invisible assets*)

Test 47

A

Verb	Personal noun	General noun	Adjective
to monopolize	–	monopoly	monopolistic
compete	competitor	competition	competitive
deregulate	–	deregulation	deregulated
to authorize	–	authority/ authorization	authorized
to legislate	legislator	legislation	legislative
to protect	protector	protection	protected
nationalize	–	nationalization	nationalized
to regulate	regulator	regulation	regulated
to partner	partner	partnership	–
to trade	trader	trade	traded/trading
to subsidize	–	subsidy	subsidized

B

1 monopoly
2 competitor
3 partnership
4 deregulate
5 trade/competition
6 regulated/protected
7 subsidized

Test 48

1 b)
2 c)
3 b)
4 a)
5 a)
6 c)

Test 49

1 a)
2 b)
3 a)
4 b)
5 a)
6 c)
7 b)
8 c)
9 a)
10 b)
11 a)
12 c)

SECTION 8: THE ECONOMIC ENVIRONMENT

Test 50

1 g)
2 d)
3 f)
4 e)
5 l)
6 h)
7 k)
8 c)
9 j)
10 b)
11 a)
12 i)

Test 51

1 International Monetary Fund
2 Organization of Petroleum Exporting Countries
3 Public Sector Borrowing Requirement
4 General Agreement on Tariffs and Trade
5 European Union
6 Gross National Product
7 Organization for Economic Co-operation and Development
8 Association of South East Asian Nations
9 International Bank for Reconstruction and Development (World Bank)
10 World Wildlife Fund
11 United Nations
12 World Health Organisation

Test 52

1 True
2 True
3 False. Not always. If consumption is high there may be more jobs in some sectors of the economy, such as retailing. However, if consumers are buying a lot of imported goods, there may be negative consequences and redundancies for domestic manufacturing.
4 False. It is most necessary during a downturn, but paying for it is more difficult for a government when income from taxation is down, and more difficult for private industry when income from sales is down.
5 False. The opposite: low taxation and low government spending.
6 True
7 False. It makes products more expensive, so less attractive, for importers.
8 True
9 False. This is gross *domestic* product (GDP). GNP *includes* companies abroad.
10 False. This is a measure of how much an industry is working to its full potential. If a company is producing only half the products that it is physically capable of producing, its capacity utilization is only 50%. This means redundancies are possible.
11 False. No. Unemployment normally rises in this case.
12 True. Generally true, but in an age of high technology, some sectors can experience high growth without creating much employment.
13 True
14 True
15 False. The term is used to describe government spending, (where government is acting on behalf of the national economy), not company spending.

Test 53

1 c)
2 e)
3 d)
4 a)
5 f)
6 b)

Test 54

1 a)
2 c)
3 b)
4 c)
5 b)
6 a)
7 b)

Test 55

1 building societies
2 interest rates
3 exchange rates
4 consumer spending
5 balance of payments
6 exports
7 deficit
8 unemployment

Test 56

1 bankers, politicians
2 inflation
3 monetary policy, exchange rates
4 high interest rates, inflation
5 small banks
6 hyper-inflation
7 the International Monetary Fund
8 disinvestment, investment fundholders

Test 57

1 monopoly
2 competitor
3 competition
4 free trade
5 export subsidies
6 economies
7 scale
8 suppliers
9 consortium
10 market share
11 subsidy
12 resources

Word List

The numbers before the entries are the tests in which they appear.

	English	Polski	Русский	Deutsch
	A			
24	abbreviated account	sprawozdanie skrócone/uproszczone	краткий отчет о финансовом положении компании	Kurzbericht
5	accidental loss	przypadkowa strata	случайный убыток	Unfallverlust
30	account	rachunek, konto	счёт	Konto
1	accountant	księgowy	бухгалтер	Bilanzbuchhalter
2	accounts	rachunki, księgi rachunkowe, sprawozdania finansowe	финансовый отчёт	Jahresabschluss
45	acquisition	nabycie, przejęcie	приобретение фирмы	Übernahme
10	administrative costs	koszty administracyjne	административные расходы	Verwaltungskosten
14, 27	advertising	reklama	реклама	Werbung
10	advertising costs	koszty reklamy	расходы на рекламу	Werbekosten
30	allowances against bills for collection	kredyty zabezpieczone nie ściągniętymi wierzytelnościami	предоставление кредита против счетов к оплате	Bewilligung gegen Inkassowechsel
45	amalgamate	dokonać fuzji/połączenia	объединяться	verschmelzen
3	analyse	analizować	анализировать	analysieren
	ASEAN (*see* Association of South East Asian Nations)			
2, 16, 19, 23, 24, 25, 43	assets	aktywa, majątek	активы	Vermögenswerte, 2; Aktiva, 16, Mittel, 19; Vermögen, 23, 24, 25; Vermögenswerte, 43
51	Association of South East Asian Nations	Stowarzyszenie Narodów Azji Południowo-Wschodniej	Ассоциация государств Юго-Восточной Азии	Verband Südostasiatischer Nationen
47	authorize	upoważniać, zezwalać	уполномочивать	bevollmächtigen, bewilligen

B

19	bad debts	nieściągalne długi	безнадёжные долги	uneinbringliche Forderungen
52, 55	balance of payments deficit	deficyt bilansu płatniczego	дефицит платёжного баланса	Zahlungsbilanzdefizite
5, 22, 23, 25, 26	balance sheet	bilans	балансовый отчет	Bilanz
1, 2, 19, 23, 25	bank	bank	банк	Bank
30	bank card	karta bankowa	банковская карточка	Servicekarte einer Bank, „Scheckkarte"
28	bank charges	opłaty bankowe	комиссионные за банковские услуги	Bankgebühren
28, 29	bank draft	trata bankowa	банковская тратта	Banktratte, Bankscheck
1	bank manager	dyrektor banku	управляющий банком	Bankdirektor
29	bank statement	wyciąg z konta	выписка с банковского счета	Kontoauszug
30	bank transfer	przelew/przekaz bankowy	банковский перевод	Überweisung
56	banker	bankier	банкир	Bankier
12, 30	banker's order	bankowe zlecenie płatnicze	банковское поручение	Zahlungs-, Überweisungsauftrag
2	bankruptcy	bankructwo, upadłość	банкротство	Insolvenz, Bankrott, Konkurs
4	bar graph	wykres słupkowy	столбцовая диаграмма	Balkendiagramm
28, 31	base rate	stopa bazowa/podstawowa	базисная ставка	Eckzins der Londoner Clearing-Banken
43, 48	bid	oferta	предложение одной компании приобрести акции другой компании	Übernahmeangebot
46	black economy	szara strefa	чёрная экономика	Schattenwirtschaft
38	blue chip	akcje renomowanych firm, pierwszorzędne papiery wartościowe	первоклассный	erstklassige Aktie, Standardpapier
38	bond	obligacja	облигация	Anleihe, Obligation
46	bonus share	akcja gratisowa	бесплатная акция	Gratisaktie
54	boom	(wysoka) koniunktura, ożywienie, boom	быстрый подъём	Hochkonjunktur, Boom, Aufschwung
31	borrow	pożyczać	занимать	einen Kredit aufnehmen
2, 23, 32, 50	borrowing	pożyczka, pożyczanie, kredyty, zadłużenie	заём, заёмные средства	Kreditaufnahme, Kredite, 23, 32; Kreditaufnahme der öffentlichen Hand, 50
52	borrowing requirement	potrzeby kredytowe	потребность в заёмных средствах	Kreditbedarf
46	bottom line	ostateczny efekt; dosł. „ostatnia linia" (najczęściej w odniesieniu do rachunku zysków i strat)	практический результат	Saldo, Zahl unter dem Strich
38	Bourse	giełda (w języku francuskim)	Парижская фондовая биржа	Börse (Paris)
25	brand name	nazwa firmowa, marka	торговая марка	Markenname

	English	Polski	Русский	Deutsch
14, 21, 57	competition	konkurencja	конкуренция	Konkurrenz; Mitbewerber
3, 43, 55	competitor	konkurent	конкурент	Mitbewerber, Konkurrent
34	comprehensive	ogólny, od wszelkiego ryzyka (polisa ubezpieczeniowa)	комбинированного страхования (полис)	(hier:) mit Vollkostenübernahme (bei Fahrzeugen: Vollkasko...)
49	conglomerate	konglomerat	конгломерат	Konglomerat, Mischkonzern
24	consolidated	skonsolidowany	консолидированный	konsolidiert
44, 57	consortium	konsorcjum	консорциум	Konsortium
3	consumer	konsument	потребитель	Verbraucher, Konsument
49, 54	consumer confidence	optymizm konsumentów	доверие покупателей	Verbraucherzuversicht
54	consumer demand	popyt na towary konsumpcyjne	потребительский спрос	Verbrauchernachfrage
52	consumer economy	koniunktura (wysokiej) konsumpcji	потребительская экономика	Verbraucherwirtschaft
53	consumer spending	wydatki konsumentów	потребительские расходы	Verbraucherausgaben
54	consumption	konsumpcja	потребление	Konsum, Verbrauch
5	contract	umowa	контракт	Vertrag, Abkommen
16, 17	contribution	pokrycie (kosztów)	валовая прибыль на единицу продукции, вклад	Deckungsbeitrag
16	contribution ratio	wskaźnik pokrycia	коэффициент выручки	Bruttogewinnspanne
7	co-operative	spółdzielnia	кооператива	Genossenschaft
9	core activity	podstawowa działalność	основной вид деятельности	Kerngeschäftsbereich
49	corporate	dotyczący dużych firm	налог на прибыль	Unternehmens... Firmen...
9, 27	cost of sales	koszt własny produkcji/sprzedaży	издержки реализации	Kosten der Verkäufe
21	cost plus	ustalenie ceny przez narzut zysku na koszty produkcji	система исчисления себестоимости товара по схеме «оптовая цена плюс вознаграждение за хранение на оптовом складе и издержки на транспорт»	Selbstkosten(ansatz)
14	cost structure	struktura kosztów	структура затрат	Kostenstruktur
8	cost, insurance, freight (c.i.f.)	koszt, ubezpieczenie i fracht	стоимость, страхование и фрахт	Kosten, Versicherung, Fracht
33, 34	cover	ubezpieczenie, zakres ubezpieczenia, ubezpieczać od	объем страховой ответственности	Versicherungsschutz, Deckung
3, 19, 31, 55	credit	kredyt, kredytowy	кредитовать, кредит, кредитный, кредит	gutschreiben, Gutschrift, Gutschrift..., Kredit, Bonität, Guthaben, Zahlungsziel,
12, 13	credit card	karta kredytowa	кредитная карточка	Kreditkarte
19	credit deficit	deficyt	кредитный дефицит	Defizit
30	credit rating	ocena zdolności kredytowej	показатель кредитоспособности	Bonitätsbeurteilung

English	Page	Polish	Russian	German
creditor	26, 30, 48	wierzyciel	кредитор	Gläubiger, Kreditor
currency	30, 50, 52	waluta, dewizowy	валюта	Währung, Währungs…
current assets	22, 23, 25, 26	aktywa bieżące, majątek obrotowy	оборотный капитал	Umlaufvermögen
current liabilities	22, 26	zobowiązania bieżące	текущие обязательства	kurzfristige Verbindlichkeiten
curve	24	krzywa	кривая	Kurve
customer	13, 14, 30	klient	покупатель, покупательский	Kunde

D

English	Page	Polish	Russian	German
damage	5	szkoda	повреждение	Schaden
data	4	data	данные	Daten
debit	3, 19	debet	дебетовать, дебет, дебетованный, дебетовый	belasten, Belastung, Belastungs…, 3; Debet…, Soll… 19
debit balance	19	saldo debetowe	дебетовое сальдо	Debetsaldo
debit card	29	karta debetowa	дебетовая карточка	Debitkarte (z.B. ec-Karte)
debt	2, 19, 22, 24, 48	dług, zadłużenie	задолженность, долг	Schuld, 2; Forderung, 19; Schuld, 22; Verschuldung, 24; Schulden, 48
debtor	22, 26	dłużnik	дебитор	Schuldner, Debitor
decline	6, 36	maleć, spadać	понизиться	nachgeben, zurückgehen, 6; Abschwung, Rückgang, 36
delivery	13	dostawa	доставка	Lieferung
demand	14, 15, 55	popyt	спрос	Nachfrage
demerger	49	podział firmy, przekształcenie części przedsiębiorstwa w odrębną firmę	разделение объединившихся ранее предприятий	Konzernentflechtung, Entfusionierung
depreciation	25, 27	amortyzacja, umorzenie, zużycie, spadek wartości	амортизация	Abschreibung
deregulate	47	ograniczać interwencję (państwa w sprawy gospodarcze), deregulować	дерегулировать	deregulieren
deteriorate	6	pogarszać się	ухудшаться	sich verschlechtern
devalue	53	dewaluować	девальвировать	abwerten
direct costs	23	koszty bezpośrednie	прямые расходы	direkte Kosten
discount	21	rabat, dyskonto	скидка	Nachlass
disinvestment	56	ograniczenie inwestycji	сокращение капиталовложений	Desinvestition, Verkauf von Anlagen
distribution	27	dystrybucja	распределение	Vertrieb, Distribution
distribution costs	10	koszty dystrybucji	издержки обращения	Vertriebskosten, Distributionskosten

	English	Polski	Русский	Deutsch
43, 45	divestiture	zbycie udziału, sprzedaż (części) firmy, dywestycja	распродажа активов	Verkauf, Veräußerung
2, 25, 26, 35	dividend	dywidenda	дивиденд	Dividende
52	domestic economy	gospodarka krajowa	внутренняя экономика	Binnenwirtschaft
4	dotted line	linia kropkowana	пунктирная линия	punktierte Linie
38	Dow Jones	Dow Jones (indeks cen akcji)	Доу-Джоунс	Dow Jones (US Aktienindex)
36	drop	spadać	падать	Rückgang
	E			
3	earn	zarabiać, przynosić dochód	зарабатывать	verdienen
24, 35	earnings	zarobki, dochód	доход	Einnahmen, Einkommen, Ertrag, Gewinn
14	economic climate	klimat gospodarczy	экономический климат	Konjunkturklima
52	economic cycle	cykl gospodarczy	экономический цикл	Konjunkturzyklus
54	economic growth	wzrost/rozwój gospodarczy	экономический рост	Wirtschaftswachstum
30	economic information	informacje gospodarcze	экономическая информация	Konjunkturdaten
6, 37	edge down	obniżać się	незначительно понизиться	allmählich sinken
52	education	kształcenie	образование	Bildung
18	electricity	energia elektryczna	электричество	Elektrizität
25	employee	pracownik	служащий	Arbeitnehmer
18	employee costs	koszty wynagrodzeń	расходы на зарплату служащим и страхование	Lohnkosten, Personalkosten
16, 25, 26	equipment	urządzenia, wyposażenie	оборудование	Geschäftsausstattung, Anlagen, Geräte
24, 43	equity	kapitał spółki, kapitał akcyjny	капитал компании, собственный капитал	Reinvermögen, 24; Aktien, 43
16, 43	equity capital	kapitał akcyjny/udziałowy/własny	собственный капитал компании	Eigenkapital
14, 34	estimate	szacować, oceniać, kosztorys	оценка, сметное предложение	Schätzung, schätzen, 14; Kostenvoranschlag, 34
	EU (*see* European Union)			
51	European Union	Unia Europejska	Европейский Союз	Europäische Union
33	excess	udział własny	эксцедент убытка	Selbstbeteiligung des Versicherungs-nehmers
50, 55, 56	exchange rate	kurs wymiany	обменный курс	Wechselkurs
45	expand	rosnąć, rozwijać się	расширяться	expandieren, sich vergrößern
5, 13, 23	expenditure	wydatki, nakłady	расходы	Aufwand, Ausgaben, Kosten

	English	Polish	Russian	German
27	expenses	koszty, wydatki	расходы	Kosten
3, 52	export	eksport	экспортировать, экспорт	Export, exportieren
54	export market	rynek eksportowy	экспортный рынок	Auslands-, Exportmarkt
3	exporter	eksporter	экспортёр	Exporteur
24	extraordinary item	operacja nadzwyczajna	непредвиденные расходы	Sonderposten, außerordentlicher Ertrag oder Aufwand

F

	English	Polish	Russian	German
37	fall back	spadać	повторно падать	zurückgehen
1	finance director	dyrektor finansowy	финансовый директор	Finanzdirektor
1	financial advisor	doradca finansowy	финансовый консультант	Finanzberater
3, 9	financial planning	planowanie finansowe	финансовое планирование	Finanzplanung
22, 26	finished goods	wyroby gotowe	готовые изделия	Fertigerzeugnisse
38	firm (v)	wzmocnić się	утвердиться	sich festigen
52	fiscal policy	polityka fiskalna	финансовая политика	Finanzpolitik
22, 23, 25, 26	fixed assets	środki trwałe, kapitał trwały	основной капитал	Sachanlagevermögen
9, 11, 16, 17, 18, 20	fixed costs	koszty stałe	постоянные издержки	Fixkosten, fixe Kosten
30	fixed interest	stałe oprocentowanie	фиксированная процентная ставка	feste Zinssätze
31	fixed rate lending	kredyty o stałym oprocentowaniu	кредитование с фиксированной процентной ставкой	Kredite zu festen Zinssätzen
43	flotation	emisja, wprowadzenie akcji spółki na giełdę	размещение	Börseneinführung
6	fluctuate	wahać się	колебаться	fluktuieren, schwanken
4	fluctuating line	krzywa wahań	скользящая линия	fluktuierende Linie
36	fluctuation	wahanie	колебание	Fluktuation, Schwankung
38	Footsie	Footsie, FTSE (indeks cen akcji)	фондовый индекс «Файнэншл таймс»	Footsie, britischer Börsenindex
12, 14, 19, 22	forecast	prognoza, przewidywany	прогнозируемый, прогноз	prognostiziert, 12; Prognose, Erwartungsrechnung, 14, 19, 22
30, 46	foreign currency	waluta obca, dewizy, dewizowy	иностранная валюта	Fremdwährungs…
30	foreign currency loans	pożyczki/kredyty w walucie obcej	займы в иностранной валюте	Devisenkredite
46	foreign currency reserves	rezerwy dewizowe	запасы иностранной валюты	Fremdwährungs-, Devisenreserven
38	Frankfurt	Frankfurt	Франкфурт	Frankfurt
57	free trade	wolny handel	свободная торговля	freier Handel
56	fundholder	inwestor (prywatny)	владелец фондовых ценностей	Investoren

	English	Polski	Русский	Deutsch
38	future	terminowa transakcja giełdowa	фьючерсный контракт	Terminkontrakt
35	futures	terminowe transakcje giełdowe, terminowy	фьючерсы	Terminkontrakthandel
	G			
39	gain	zyskać, rosnąć	повышаться	Kursgewinn
	GATT (*see* General Agreement on Tariffs and Trade)			
	GDP (*see* Gross Domestic Product)			
16	gearing	dźwignia finansowa	соотношение между собственными и привлеченными средствами компании	Verhältnis zwischen Fremd- und Eigenkapital
51	General Agreement on Tariffs and Trade	Układ Ogólny w Sprawie Taryf Celnych i Handlu	Общее соглашение о тарифах и торговле	das internationale Zoll- und Handelsabkommen
6	get better	poprawiać się	улучшаться	sich verbessern
	GNP (*see* Gross National Product)			
19	go bankrupt	zbankrutować	стать банкротом	in Konkurs gehen
48	go into liquidation	likwidować się, przechodzić w stan likwidacji	подвергнуться ликвидации	in Konkurs gehen
6	go up	iść w górę	возрастать	steigen
46	government securities	państwowe/rządowe papiery wartościowe	правительственные ценные бумаги	Staatstitel, Staatspiere
50, 52	government spending	wydatki publiczne	государственные расходы	Staatsausgaben, öffentliche Investitionen
	GPP's (*see* Group Pension Plans)			
24	gross	brutto	валовый	Brutto
49	Gross Domestic Product	produkt krajowy brutto	валовый внутренний продукт	Bruttoinlandsprodukt
51, 52	Gross National Product	produkt narodowy brutto	валовый национальный продукт	Bruttosozialprodukt
9, 16, 27	gross profit margin	zysk brutto, marża zysku brutto	маржа валовой прибыли	Bruttogewinnspanne
42	Group Pension Plans	grupowe programy emerytalne	Системы пенсионного обеспечения служащих	GPP (Versicherungsangebot für Altersvorsorge mit Arbeitgeberunterstützung)
35, 42, 49, 53	growth	wzrost, rozwój	рост	Wachstum
3	guarantee	gwarancja, gwarantować	гарантия	Garantie, garantieren

	English	Polski	Русский	Deutsch
2, 23, 31, 35	interest	odsetki, oprocentowanie	проценты	Zinsen
27	interest payment	odsetki	выплата процентов	Zinszahlung
31, 50, 55	interest rate	stopa procentowa	процентная ставка	Zinssatz
46	interim dividend	dywidenda tymczasowa/zaliczkowa	промежуточный дивиденд	Zwischendividende, Interimsdividende
51	International Bank for Reconstruction and Development	Międzynarodowy Bank Odbudowy i Rozwoju	Международный банк реконструкции и развития	Internationale Bank für Wiederaufbau und Entwicklung
51, 56	International Monetary Fund	Międzynarodowy Fundusz Walutowy	Международный валютный фонд	Internationaler Währungsfonds
3, 26, 41	invest	inwestować	инвестировать	investieren, anlegen
24, 25, 35, 40, 46, 52	investment	inwestycja, nakłady	инвестиции	Investition, Anlage
41	investment trust	trust inwestycyjny	инвестиционная компания	Investmentfonds, Kapitalanlagegesellschaft
3, 41	investor	inwestor	инвестор	Investor, Anleger
50	invisible earnings	dochód niewidoczny, dochód z pozycji pozataworowych	поступления от невидимых статей	Einkünfte aus unsichtbaren Geschäftstransaktionen
22	invoice (v)	fakturować	инвойсировать	in Rechnung stellen
22	invoiced sales	transakcje fakturowane, sprzedaż fakturowana	инвойсированные продажи	fakturierter Umsatz
42	ISA (Individual Savings Account)	ISA (w Wielkiej Brytanii: osobisty rachunek oszczędnościowy z ulgami podatkowymi)	Специальный счёт сбережений, не облагаемых налогом (в Великобритании)	ISA (privates Vorsorgekonzept)
46	issue price	cena emisyjna	цена при выпуске	Emissionskurs
J				
54	job market	rynek pracy	рынок труда	Arbeitsmarkt
52	job	praca, zawód, etat, posada	работа	Stelle, Arbeitsplatz
43	joint venture	spółka joint-venture	совместное предприятие	Joint Venture
44	joint-venture agreement	umowa joint-venture	договор о совместном предприятии	Joint-Venture-Abkommen
L				
11	labour	robocizna	труд	Lohn..., Personal... (z.B. -kosten)
10, 52	labour costs	koszty robocizny	затраты на труд	Lohnkosten, Personalkosten

	English	Polish	Russian	German
25, 26	land	ziemia, grunty, nieruchomości gruntowe	земля	Grundstücke
18	leasing	leasing	лизинг	Leasing, Miet-, Pacht-,
34	legal costs	koszty sądowe	судебные издержки	Rechtskosten
47	legislation	ustawodawstwo, legislacja	законодательство	Gesetzgebung
5, 30	letter of credit	akredytywa	аккредитив	Akkreditiv
2, 16, 22, 23, 24, 25	liabilities	pasywa, zobowiązania	обязательства	Verbindlichkeiten, Passiva
25	licence	licencja	лицензия	Lizenz
33	life assurance	ubezpieczenie na życie	страхование жизни	Lebensversicherung
11	lighting	oświetlenie	освещение	Licht, Beleuchtung
8	Limited	z ograniczoną odpowiedzialnością (spółka)	Лимитед	(Gesellschaft) mit beschränkter Haftung
4	line graph	wykres liniowy	линейный график	Liniengrafik, -diagramm
19, 24, 25	liquid assets	aktywa płynne, środki płynne	ликвидные активы	flüssige Mittel
19, 26, 48	liquidation	likwidacja	ликвидация	Liquidation, Konkurs
19, 22, 25, 30	liquidity	likwidacja; upłynnienie płynność	ликвидность	Liquidität
13, 19, 28, 30, 31	loan	pożyczka, kredyt	ссуда, заём	Kredit, Darlehen
19, 34	loss	strata	убыток	Verlust
34	loss adjuster	dyspaszer	диспашер по убыткам	Schadenregulierer
	Ltd (see Limited)			

M

	English	Polish	Russian	German
44	management	kierowanie	управление	Leitung
11, 54	manufacturing	produkcja	производство, выпуск	Herstellungs…
54	manufacturing output	wielkość/poziom produkcji	выпуск продукции обрабатывающей промышленности	Industrieproduktion
15, 17, 31	margin	marża	маржа	Marge, Spanne
21	marginal costs	koszty krańcowe	предельные издержки	Grenzkosten
14, 21, 30	market	rynek, rynkowy	рынок, рыночный	Markt
1	market analyst	analityk rynku	специалист по исследованию рынка	Marktanalytiker
57	market forces	siły rynkowe	рыночные силы	Marktkräfte
21	market price	cena rynkowa	рыночная цена	Marktpreis
21, 36	market share	udział w rynku	рыночная доля	Marktanteil

	English	Polski	Русский	Deutsch
14	marketing	marketing	маркетинг	Marketing
32	marketing plan	plan marketingowy	план сбыта	Marketingplan
12	master budget	budżet główny, plan całkowity	главный бюджет	Gesamtbudget
33	medical	ubezpieczenie od kosztów leczenia	медицинский	medizinisch, (hier:) Kranken(versicherung)
3	merge	łączyć (się)	объединяться	fusionieren
43, 45	merger	fuzja	объединение	Fusion
56	monetary policy	polityka monetarna/pieniężna/walutowa	денежно-кредитная политика	Geldpolitik
13	money	pieniądze	деньги	Geld
45, 47, 57	monopoly	monopol	монополия	Monopol
2	mortgage	kredyt hipoteczny	ипотека	Hypothek
18	mortgage payment	spłata kredytu hipotecznego	ипотечный платёж	Hypothekenrückzahlung, -tilgung
41	mutual fund	fundusz wzajemny	инвестиционная компания открытого типа	Investmentfonds

N

	English	Polski	Русский	Deutsch
50	National Debt	dług publiczny, dług państwowy	государственный долг	Staatsschuld
47	nationalize	nacjonalizować, upaństwawiać	национализировать	verstaatlichen
26	net assets	aktywa netto, wartość aktywów netto	чистая сумма активов	Nettovermögen
26	net current assets	aktywa bieżące, środki obrotowe netto	чистые текущие активы	Nettoumlaufvermögen
22	net income	dochód netto	чистый доход	Nettoeinkommen
16	net profit	zysk netto	чистая прибыль	Nettogewinn
9	net profit margin	zysk netto, marża zysku netto	коэффициент прибыльности	Nettoumsatzrendite, Nettogewinnspanne
23	net sales	sprzedaż/obrót netto	чистая сумма продаж	Nettoumsatz
38	New York Stock Exchange	giełda nowojorska	Фондовая биржа в Нью-Йорке	New Yorker Börse
29	night safe	nocny sejf	ночной сейф (для сдачи денег в банк без участия персонала)	Nachttresor
34	no claims bonus	zniżka za bezszkodowość	скидка на безаварийность	Schadenfreiheitsrabatt
14	non-regular business	nieregularni klienci	нерегулярный бизнес	keine Stammkundschaft. Neukunden

O

OECD (*see* Organisation for Economic Co-operation and Development)

OEIC, Open-Ended Investment Company (*see* Open-Ended Investment Vehicle)

OPEC (*see* Organisation of Petroleum Exporting Nations)

41	Open-Ended Investment Vehicle	produkt inwestycyjny typu otwartego	Открытый инвестиционный механизм	offener Investmentfonds
23	opening balance	saldo początkowe/otwarcia	начальное сальдо	Eröffnungsbilanz
24	operating income	dochody operacyjne	производственная прибыль	Betriebseinkommen, betrieblicher Ertrag
19	opportunity cost	koszt utraconych korzyści/możliwości	потери в результате неиспользованного альтернативного курса	Opportunitätskosten, Nutzungsentgang
26	ordinary share	akcja zwykła	обыкновенная акция	Stammaktie
51	Organisation for Economic Co-operation and Development	Organizacja Współpracy Gospodarczej i Rozwoju	Организация экономического сотрудничества и развития	Organisation für wirtschaftliche Zusammenarbeit und Entwicklung
51	Organisation of Petroleum Exporting Nations	Organizacja Państw Eksporterów Ropy Naftowej	Организация стран-экспортёров нефти	Verband der erdölexportierenden Länder
49	overcapacity	nadwyżka zdolności produkcyjnych	избыточная мощность	Überkapazität
25, 26, 28, 30, 31	overdraft	przekroczenie stanu konta, kredyt przejściowy	кредит по текущему счёту (овердрафт)	(hier:) Bankdarlehen 25, 26; Kreditrahmen, Überziehung, 28, 31
30	overdraft facility	kredyt przejściowy, kredyt w rachunku bieżącym	предоставление овердрафта	Überziehungsmöglichkeit, Dispositionskredit
19	overdraft payment	spłata kredytu przejściowego	платежи по овердрафту	Rückführung eines Überziehungskredits
9, 13, 16, 18, 27	overheads	koszty stałe/ogólne	накладные расходы	Gemeinkosten
43	ownership	własność	владение	Besitz

P

P & L account (*see* profit and loss account)

p/e ratio (*see* price/earnings ratio)

43, 44	parent company	spółka macierzysta	материнская компания	Muttergesellschaft
44	partially-owned	kontrolowane częściowo	с частичным владением	teilweise im Besitz stehen von
7, 44, 47	partnership	spółka	партнёрство (товарищество)	Personengesellschaft, 7, 44; Personengesellschaft, Partnerschaft, 47
25	patent	patent	патент	Patent

	English	Polski	Русский	Deutsch
8	Pay As You Earn	potrącanie z wynagrodzeń zaliczek na podatek dochodowy	«Заработал – плати» (система удержания подоходного налога из заработной платы)	Einbehaltung der Einkommenssteuer, Quellenabzug durch den Arbeitgeber (in Großbritannien)
	PAYE (*see* Pay As You Earn)			
28	payee	odbiorca płatności	ремиттент	Zahlungsempfänger, Begünstiger
29	paying-in slip	odcinek wpłaty	платёжная расписка	Einzahlungsschein
13	payment	płatność	платёж	Zahlung
21	penetration strategy	strategia penetracji (rynku)	стратегия проникновения	Penetrationsstrategie
2, 40	pension	emerytura	пенсия	Pension, Rente
	PEP (*see* Personal Equity Plan)			
42	Personal Equity Plan	PEP (w Wielkiej Brytanii: plan lokat kapitałowych dla osób prywatnych)	Программа финансовых инвестиций (в Великобритании)	PEP (auf Aktien basierendes staatliches Vermögensbildungsprogramm)
40	personal investment	inwestycje osób prywatnych	финансовые инвестиции	Privatinvestition
4	pie chart	wykres kołowy	секторная диаграмма	Kreisdiagramm
26	plant	wyposażenie	основные производственные средства	Maschinen
	PLC or plc (*see* Public Limited Company)			
33, 34	policy	polisa	страховой полис	Versicherungspolice
35, 40	portfolio	portfel	портфель	Portefeuille
26	preference shares	akcja uprzywilejowana	привилегированные акции	Vorzugsaktie
33, 34	premium	składka, stawka	страховой взнос	Versicherungsprämie
24	pre-tax	przed opodatkowaniem	до уплаты налогов	vor Steuerabzug
23, 27	pre-tax profit	zysk przed opodatkowaniem	прибыль до вычета налогов	Gewinn vor Steuerabzug
11, 14, 15	price	cena	цена	Preis
36, 44	price war	wojna cenowa	ценовая война	Preiskrieg
8	price/earnings ratio	wskaźnik cena/zysk	соотношение цен и заработка	Kurs-Gewinn-Verhältnis
15	price-demand	relacja cena-popyt	цена-спрос	Preis-Nachfrage.../Absatz...
14, 21	pricing policy	polityka cenowa	ценовая политика	Preispolitik
57	private capital	kapitał prywatny	частный капитал	Privatkapital
44	private company	spółka prywatna/osobowa	частная компания	Privatgesellschaft, Personengesellschaft
7	private limited company	prywatna spółka z ograniczoną odpowiedzialnością	частная компания с ограниченной ответственностью	(vergleichbar:) GmbH
3	produce	produkować, wytwarzać	производить	produzieren, herstellen
11, 19	production	produkcja	производство	Produktion, Herstellung

	English	Polish	Russian	German
10	production costs	koszty produkcji	издержки производства	Produktionskosten
18	professional fee	opłaty za usługi obce	расходы, связанные с услугами специалистов	Honorar
18	professional indemnity insurance	ubezpieczenie od odpowiedzialności zawodowej	страхование профессиональной ответственности	Berufshaftpflichtversicherung
2, 9, 15, 17, 20, 23, 25	profit	zysk	прибыль	Gewinn, 2, 9, 15, 17, 23, 25; im Gewinnbereich, 20
5, 8, 22, 23, 27	Profit and Loss account	rachunek zysków i strat, rachunek wyników	счёт прибылей и убытков	Gewinn- und Verlustrechnung
9, 22	profitability	rentowność	рентабельность	Rentabilität
32	projection	prognoza	прогноз	Prognose
14	promotion	promocja	реклама	Werbe…, Verkaufsförderung
23, 25, 26	property	nieruchomość/nieruchomości	имущество	Immobilien
47	protection	ochrona	защита	Schutz
	PSBR (*see* Public Sector Borrowing Requirement)			
7, 8, 38	Public Limited Company/public limited company	spółka akcyjna	публичная компания с ограниченной ответственностью	Aktiengesellschaft
50, 51	Public Sector Borrowing Requirement	potrzeby kredytowe sektora państwowego	потребности государственного сектора в заёмных средствах	Kreditbedarf der öffentlichen Hand
50	public spending	wydatki publiczne	государственные расходы	Ausgaben der öffentlichen Hand

R

	English	Polish	Russian	German
37	rally	iść w górę, zwyżkować	повышаться	sich erholen
52	rationalization	racjonalizacja	рационализация	Rationalisierung
45	rationalize	racjonalizować, restrukturyzować	рационализировать	rationalisieren
11, 26	raw materials	surowce	сырьё	Rohstoffe
6	reach a peak	osiągnąć szczyt/maksimum	достигать высшей точки	den Höhepunkt/Höchststand erreichen
52	real terms	rzeczywisty, realny	реальное выражение	preisbereinigte Größe
48	receiver	syndyk (masy upadłościowej), likwidator	ликвидатор (официальное лицо, назначенное судом для ликвидации неплатёжеспособной компании)	Konkursverwalter
6	recover	wychodzić z kryzysu	достичь прежнего уровня	sich erholen
36	recovery	ożywienie	восстановление	Erholung
41	redeem	wykupić	выкупать	zurücknehmen

English		Polski	Русский	Deutsch
25	regular costs	koszty regularne	постоянные издержки	regelmäßige Kosten
14	regular customers	stali klienci	постоянные покупатели	Stammkunden
47	regulator	organ nadzoru/kontroli/regulacji (rynku)	регулятор	Aufsichtsbehörde
11	rent	czynsz	арендная плата	Miete
32	repayment	spłata	погашение	Rückzahlung, Tilgung
19, 48	reschedule payments	przekładać termin spłat	реконструировать платежи	umfinanzieren, umschulden
57	resources	zasoby, środki	ресурсы	Ressourcen, Mittel
48	restructuring	restrukturyzacja	реструктуризация	Umstrukturierung
51, 53	retail price	cena detaliczna	розничная цена	Einzelhandelspreis
53, 54	retail sales	sprzedaż detaliczna	розничные продажи	Einzelhandelsumsätze
46	retail price index	indeks cen detalicznych	индекс розничных цен	Einzelhandelspreisindex
16	retained profit	zysk nie rozliczony/nie podzielony	нераспределённая прибыль	einbehaltener Gewinn
35	return	zwrot, zysk	доход, доходность	Rendite
17, 24	revenue	przychody, dochód	доход	Einkünfte, Einnahmen
38, 48	rights issue	emisja praw poboru akcji	выпуск обыкновенных акций для размещения среди уже существующих акционеров	Bezugsrechtsemission
6	rise	rosnąć, podnosić się	повышаться	steigen
33	risk	ryzyko	риск	Risiko
4	row	wiersz	строка	Zeile
S				
9	sales	sprzedaż	продажи	Umsatz, Verkäufe
14	sales force	pracownicy działu sprzedaży i przedstawiciele handlowi	торговый персонал	Verkaufsaußendienst
14	sales forecaster	osoba odpowiedzialna za prognozowanie obrotów	прогноз сбыта	jemand, der eine Absatzprognose erstellt
14	sales forecasting	prognozowanie sprzedaży/obrotów	прогнозирование сбыта	Erstellen von Absatzprognosen
27	sales income	przychody ze sprzedaży	поступления от продаж	Umsatzerlös
23	sales record	ewidencja sprzedaży, dane na temat sprzedaży	торговый учёт	Umsatzzahlen
14	sales volume	wielkość/poziom/wolumen obrotów/sprzedaży	объём реализованной продукции	Umsatzvolumen

28	savings bank	kasa oszczędnościowa	сберегательный банк	Sparkasse, -institut (nicht mit den „Sparkassen" in D zu vergleichen)
33	schedule	plan ubezpieczenia	график погашения	Versicherungsaufstellung mit Zahlungsaufforderung, Versicherungsplan
14	seasonal influence	czynnik sezonowy	сезонное воздействие	saisonbedingter Einfluss
14	seasonal variation	różnice sezonowe	сезонные колебания	saisonbedingte Variation
30, 32	security	zabezpieczenie	ценная бумага, залог	Sicherheit
4	segment	segment, część	доля	Segment, Teil
9, 10	selling costs	koszty sprzedaży	торговые издержки	Verkaufskosten, Vertriebskosten
16	selling price	cena sprzedaży	запродажная цена	Verkaufspreis
49	sell-off	sprzedaż (spółki zależnej)	распродажа	Veräußerung, Verkauf
9	setting-up costs	koszty organizacji	затраты на наладочные работы	Gründungskosten, Anlaufkosten
31	setting-up fee	opłata od umowy kredytowej	плата за открытие овердрафта	Einrichtungsgebühr
1, 2, 26, 35, 38, 46	share	akcja, udział	акция	Aktie, Anteil
26, 43	share capital	kapitał akcyjny	акционерный капитал	Aktienkapital
5	share certificate	certyfikat akcji	акционерный сертификат	Aktienzertifikat
36, 39	share price	cena akcji	цена акции	Aktienkurs
49	share value	wartość akcji, wartość rynkowa 49	стоимость акции	Aktienkurs
25, 26, 48	shareholder	akcjonariusz, udziałowiec	акционер	Aktionär
6	shrink	maleć	сокращаться	schrumpfen
43	sister company	przedsiębiorstwo „siostrzane"	сестринская компания	Schwestergesellschaft
21	skimming strategy	strategia „zbierania śmietanki"	стратегия «снимания сливок»	Gewinnabschöpfungsstrategie
54	slowdown	osłabienie koniunktury, zwolnienie tempa wzrostu (gospodarczego)	спад	Rückgang
49	soar	gwałtownie wzrosnąć	резко увеличиваться	rapide/steigen
7	sole trader	przedsiębiorca indywidualny	единоличный торговец	Einzelkaufmann
4	solid line	linia ciągła	непрерывная линия	durchgehende Linie
43	stake	udział	доля	Kapitaleinlage, Beteiligung
28, 30	standing order	stałe zlecenie płatnicze	распоряжение о регулярных платежах	Dauerauftrag
28	statement	wyciąg	выписка со счёта	Kontoauszug
30	status enquiry	badanie sytuacji finansowej	запрос о финансовом положении	Anfrage bei der Kreditauskunft
6	stay the same	pozostawać bez zmian	остаться на прежнем уровне	unverändert/gleich bleiben
37	steady	ustabilizować się	устойчивый	fest, stabil
37	step out	wzrosnąć, pójść w górę	выходить за пределы	steigen, anziehen

101

	English	Polski	Русский	Deutsch
1, 21, 22, 25, 26, 35, 43, 46	stock	kapitał akcyjny, papiery wartościowe; zapasy, inwentarz, stan (magazynu)	акция	Aktie, 1; Lagerbestand, 21, 22; unfertige Waren, 25; Waren, Vorräte 26; Waren/Wertpapiere, 35; Aktienkapital, 43, 46
38, 42	stock exchange	giełda papierów wartościowych	фондовая биржа	Börse
54	stock level	poziom zapasów, stan inwentarza	уровень запасов	Lagerbestand(sniveau)
5	stock value	wartość akcji	цена акции	Aktienwert
1	stockbroker	makler giełdowy	биржевой брокер	Börsenmakler
10	storage costs	koszty magazynowania	стоимость хранения запасов	Lagerkosten
44	sub-contractor	podwykonawca	субподрядчик	Subkontraktor, Unterauftragnehmer
11, 44, 45	subsidiary	spółka zależna	дочерняя фирма	Tochtergesellschaft
57	subsidy	subwencja, subsydium, dotacja	субсидия	Subvention
19, 25, 30	supplier	dostawca	поставщик	Lieferant
52	supply	podaż	поставлять	Angebot

T

	English	Polski	Русский	Deutsch
4	table	tabela	таблица	Tabelle
43, 45	takeover	przejęcie	покупка одной компанией контрольного пакета акций другой	Übernahme
2, 23, 26	tax	podatek	налог	Steuern
42	tax advantage	korzyść podatkowa	выгода, обеспечиваемая системой налогового обложения	Steuervorteil
25, 46	tax authorities	władze skarbowe	налоговые власти	Steuerbehörde
1	tax consultant	doradca podatkowy	налоговый консультант	Steuerberater
1	tax inspector	inspektor podatkowy	инспектор налогов	Steuerprüfer
1	tax return	deklaracja/zeznanie podatkowe	налоговая декларация	Steuererklärung
52	taxation	opodatkowanie	налогообложение	Besteuerung
29	teller	kasjer(ka)	кассир	Kassierer(in)
5, 44	tender	oferta przetargowa, składać ofertę	тендер	Angebot
33	term	okres	срок действия	Laufzeit
50	tertiary sector	trzeci sektor; sektor usług	обслуживающий сектор	tertiärer Sektor, Dienstleistungsindustrie
33	third party	osoba trzecia; od odpowiedzialności cywilnej (ubezpieczenie)	третье лицо	Haftpflicht…
32	track record	osiągnięcia, reputacja	послужной список	zurückliegende Unternehmensergebnisse

102

		handel, handlować	торговать, торговля, торговый, осуществлять торговлю	Handel treiben, Handel, 3; handeln, 41;
3, 41, 47	trade			Handel, 47
49, 54	trade deficit	deficyt bilansu handlowego	торговый дефицит	Handelsdefizit
30	trade development	rozwój handlu	развитие торговли	Handelsentwicklung
49	trade surplus	dodatni bilans handlowy	активное сальдо торгового баланса	Handelsüberschuss
25, 46	trade mark	znak handlowy	торговая марка	Warenzeichen
46, 47	trading	handlowy	торгующий	Handels…
50, 52	training	szkolenie, doskonalenie zawodowe	профессиональное обучение	Ausbildung
41	transaction cost	koszt transakcji	трансакционные издержки	Umsatzgebühren, Transaktionskosten
6, 54	trend	trend	тенденция	Trend, Tendenz
41	trust law	prawo o funduszach powierniczych/trustach inwestycyjnych	закон об инвестиционных трастах	Gesetz in Bezug auf die Verwaltung von Treuhandvermögen
2, 9, 12, 15, 16, 22	turnover	obrót	оборот	Umsatz

U

	UN (see United Nations)			
31	unauthorized overdraft fee	opłata za nieuzgodnione przekroczenie stanu konta	плата за неразрешённый овердрафт	Gebühr für eine nicht bewilligte/vereinbarte Überziehung
4	undulating line	linia falująca	волнистая линия	wellenförmige Linie
50, 52, 54	unemployment	bezrobocie	безработица	Arbeitslosigkeit
16, 17	unit contribution	jednostkowe pokrycie (kosztów)	выручка на единицу продукции	pro Einheit erbrachter Deckungsbeitrag
41	unit trust	trust inwestycyjny	паевой траст	offener Investmentfonds
51	United Nations	Organizacja Narodów Zjednoczonych	Объединённые нации	Vereinte Nationen

V

25, 27	value	wartość	стоимость	Wert
8	Value Added Tax	podatek od wartości dodanej, podatek od towarów i usług	Налог на добавленную стоимость	Mehrwertsteuer
11, 16, 17, 20	variable costs	koszty zmienne	переменные издержки	variable Kosten
	VAT (see Value Added Tax)			
4	vertical axis	oś pionowa	вертикальная ось	vertikale Achse
14	volume of sales	wielkość/poziom/wolumen sprzedaży	объем реализованной продукции	Umsatzvolumen

English	Polski	Русский	Deutsch
W			
55 wage	płaca	заработная плата	Lohn
16, 19, 52 wealth	majątek, bogactwo, dobrobyt	материальные ценности, благосостояние	Vermögen
WHO (*see* World Health Organization)			
44 wholly-owned	(spółka zależna) kontrolowana w 100%	полностью принадлежащий материнской компании	hundertprozentig(e) (Tochtergesellschaft)
29 withdrawal	wypłata, pobranie (pieniędzy)	снятие денег со счёта	Abhebung
11 worker	pracownik, robotnik	рабочий	Arbeiter
26 working capital	kapitał obrotowy	оборотный капитал	Betriebskapital
16, 22, 26 work-in-progress	produkcja w toku	незавершённое производство	unfertige Erzeugnisse/Leistungen
51 World Health Organization	Światowa Organizacja Zdrowia	Всемирная организация здравоохранения	Weltgesundheitsorganisation
49 write-off (a debt)	odpisać, wyksięgować (dług)	списывать	(eine Schuld) abschreiben

15128   3626